From the Pope to Pigeons;

From Dreams to Heaven

– Twenty Essays and Anecdotes

By

Michael J. Lowis

OTHER TITLES BY MICHAEL J. LOWIS

The Gospel Miracles: What Really Happened?

Euthanasia, Suicide, and Despair: Can the Bible Help?

Ageing Disgracefully, With Grace

Twenty Years in South Africa: An Immigrant's Tale

What do we know about God? Evidence from the

Hebrew Scriptures

Reincarnation: An Historical Novel Spanning 4,000

years

Contents

Preface

It has been said that everyone has a story to tell, or even a whole book inside them. We each live a unique life, and have experiences that are not shared by anyone else. Tackling a whole volume might be a daunting task for some people, although an autobiography would always be of interest to family members, and especially to generations further down the line. I would love to know more about my ancestors, but alas, none of them thought to record their lives on paper.

Thus, whilst a lengthy book might be impractical for many, we all love to tell others about specific episodes in our lives, and hence short stories could be an option. In addition, we might have known some interesting characters whose exploits could be recorded, or questions of our own that we wish to share with others. Once the writing is set in motion, it is surprising how one idea follows another.

This is the way the present book came to be. Firstly there were some significant or amusing experiences that needed recording, and then some observations about the world in which we live were worth a chapter. In addition, several interesting topics were investigated during my life as an academic, and the findings from these are now shared with you, the reader. Before many moons had passed, there were enough individual articles to complete this modest tome of twenty chapters.

What is contained within these pages is a gallimaufry, or hotchpotch, of topics that includes memoire, narratives, research reports, anecdotes, and advice on living a happy life. All of them are non-fiction; there are no fantasy tales here, although a touch of imagination did enter into one of them – 'Pigeon talk'. My hope is that you, dear reader, will find something of interest in what has been written. Also, if you have not tried to record your thoughts, experiences and observations yet, maybe you will now be inspired to do so.

- -

Chapter 1

The day the Pope saved my life

No doubt we have all had a day that we shall never forget, maybe one that was life-changing. The most memorable incident for me occurred on 30th September, 1979, and it involved the pope of that time – albeit indirectly.

Pope John Paul ll was the first non-Italian in more than 400 years to attain this office. His real name was Karol Józef Wojyla; he was born in Poland in 1920, and ordained in 1964. Three years later, Pope Paul Vl made Wojyla a cardinal and, in 1978, he succeeded his predecessor John Paul l and became the 264th pope. During his tenure he was a popular and charismatic leader of the Catholic Church, and an active campaigner for human rights. Despite his popularity, in 1981 John Paul was the victim of an assassination attempt, whilst in St. Peter's Square in Vatican City. Although being shot four times, he made a successful recovery.

The motivation for this vicious act is not known, but some believe it may have been because of his support of solidarity in his home country of Poland, at a time of attempted communist domination. Amazingly, in the following year, he was attacked again. It occurred in Fatima, Portugal, and was carried out by a fanatical priest. On this occasion the pope received several knife wounds, but again he fortunately recovered. John Paul was believed to have suffered from Parkinson's disease in his later years, and he in died in Italy in 2005, aged 84.

During his time in office, he travelled widely to spread his message of faith and peace. It was fortunate for me that, on 30th September, 1979, this included his visit to Ireland, the first ever made to that country by a pope. At this time I was employed by an international pharmaceuticals company. Auditors from the American headquarters had invited me to join them in a quality inspection of their manufacturing facility in Castlebar, which is situated in County Mayo, to the north-west of Ireland.

The leader of the audit team and I met up in London, and the next morning we flew by scheduled aircraft to Shannon airport. Once there, the intention was that we would be joined by two other auditors, who would have flown in from the USA. This was the very day of the pope's historic visit. He had just arrived in Dublin, and television screens had been placed all around the airport lounge. They relayed every moment of the event to passengers who had the opportunity to linger for a while. The two of us had time to watch some of this coverage, whilst awaiting the arrival of our colleagues, and it was obvious that the event had generated widespread enthusiasm and euphoria.

All the streets were lined with bunting, which included the distinctive yellow papal flags. There was an opportunity later for me to buy one of these as a souvenir, and it is still in my possession to remind me of this significant day in my life. The plan was that, once the others had arrived, the four of us would complete the journey to the factory in a small aircraft that had been chartered for this purpose.

Things then started to go wrong. The rest of the audit team were not on the flight that arrived from the USA. When this became clear, the team leader said that our chartered aircraft could not be delayed. The two of us would have to complete the journey alone. Assuming that the other auditors arrived on a later plane, they would then have to join us by whatever means they could.

We boarded our private transport, and the pilot took off without delay. By this time, Pope John Paul was either on his way to, or had just arrived at, the small town of Knock, to conduct one of the main masses of his visit. This urban area is conveniently situated close to the centre of Southern Ireland, and it was later estimated that 450,000 people had attended the event, which represented over thirteen percent of the entire population of that country. As might be expected, the level of security was very high: not only were there road blocks all around Knock, but no aircraft were permitted to fly over the town whilst the pope was present.

Our original flight plan was to fly north, passing over Knock, and land on a short grass landing strip next to the Castlebar factory. Shortly after take-off, the pilot announced, "Because of the flight restrictions, our course would now have to take a westward loop over the sea, and then turn back toward the land for our approach to the factory runway. The flight would therefore take about twenty minutes longer than it would have done on the direct route." Although we were not particularly happy with this delay we appreciated the reason, and just resigned ourselves to a longer journey.

Despite the drizzle on the windows, and the rather ominous view of the boiling sea beneath us, we had an uneventful journey until we were on the approach to the landing strip. Our pilot then made another announcement: "The weather has suddenly deteriorated, a mist was closing in, and visibility is poor." What followed was news that we certainly did not want to hear: "Because the landing strip is unmanned, there is no radar or other guidance system. In the interests of safety, there is no alternative but to turn around and return to Shannon airport." It was little consolation when he added that, had we been able to follow the original flight plan, there would have been just enough time for him to land, let us alight, and then take off before the weather closed in.

You can imagine how we felt about this, but obviously we had to accept the situation. After a tedious return journey, we eventually approached Shannon and touched down. A few seconds later, as the pilot started to apply the brakes, the plane started to shake violently. It was so strong that some of the instruments jumped out of their sockets. He released the brakes and the aircraft steadied, but the shaking began again whenever he tried to slow down.

The pilot then radioed the control tower saying that, because of the instability when he tried to use the brakes, he would have to freewheel until the plane came to a natural halt. Fortunately, the Shannon runway is one of the longest in the British Isles, and the air traffic controller ensured that no other aircraft tried to land behind us. After what seemed to be an age, but in reality was probably only a minute, we eventually came to a stop. Wondering what we would discover, we got out and looked to see if we could see what had gone wrong.

The pilot pointed out that the supporting structure for the front wheel mounting had broken, so that every time the brakes were applied the plane tipped forward and became unstable. He said it was just lucky that the runway was long enough to let him freewheel to a stop. If he had been able to attempt a landing at the very short factory airstrip, the plane would have either somersaulted when the brakes were applied, or crashed into buildings at the end of the grass strip. There would not have been an opportunity to either taxi to a halt, or try and take off again. Either way, we would have been very lucky to escape with our lives.

The reality is this started to sink in. If we had not been delayed flying over the sea to avoid Knock where the pope was, we would have attempted a landing on the strip next to the factory – with disastrous consequences. Were we just lucky? Was this only a coincidence? Or was it meant to be that John Paul was there for us just when we needed him?

There is a postscript to this story, as what followed later was as meaningful for me as was the narrowly-avoided accident, but in a completely different way. By the time we had returned at Shannon, the other two auditors had arrived from the USA on a later plane. The leader said we had no alternative but to take a taxi for the quite long drive up to the hotel in County Mayo.

It was now late in the afternoon. My feelings at that time comprised a rather confused mixture of, on the one hand, the nervy after-effects of our earlier adventure and, on the other, being fed up that we would be cramped up in a taxi for an extended journey. It was still drizzling, and also getting dark; many roads remained closed because of the pope's presence. It was going to be a miserable journey. Could it get any worse, I wondered?

We came up against the first road block as we approached the outskirts of Knock, which was still in a state of high security. Were we about to be told to turn around and only try again several hours later? The taxi driver impressed us with his skill at being able to convince the police that we were not a security risk, and that we just wanted to proceed to our ultimate destination as quickly as possible. Bravo for him!

It was not long before my earlier silent question was answered by the team leader – yes, it could get worse! He had been to our Castlebar hotel before, so he knew how it operated. "We would arrive too late for dinner", he said, adding with small comfort, "but I hope that the proprietor will be able to rustle up a sandwich or something before we go to bed." This certainly did nothing to raise the spirits. At long last, in the dark, we turned into the grounds of the hotel. Looming up ahead of us was the outline of a building that could have been used for the film *"Psycho."* I don't think it would have been possible to be filled with more doom and gloom about what was surely in store for us.

But then, as we drew up to the building, a door opened revealing a bright, almost ethereal light. A man came out to the car and gave us a warm welcome, saying that he realized we would be late and that he had delayed dinner until our arrival. We were ushered inside, and into the cheerful dining room with a long table already filling up with food and bottles of wine. The transformation from being at the lowest ebb to a feeling of joy and happiness was instant, and one of the most remarkable transformations of my life – a genuine epiphany! It was a wonderful meal that included local salmon, and there was good company and laughter. A truly remarkable day, but one that would not have ended happily without Pope John Paul ll. Indeed, it was a day I shall never forget.

(Note: A version of this memoire was previously published in my book 'Twenty Years In South Africa'. It is used here by permission of Wipf and Stock Publishers. www.wipfandstock.com)

Chapter 2

Pigeon talk

Have you ever lain awake in bed, just as the sun was rising, and heard the pigeons talking to each other? During that bleary-eyed state between sleeping and waking, it is easy to quickly forget what may have been revealed during such eavesdropping. If you want to record these conversations, you need to keep a paper and pencil on your bedside table. Once the small-talk begins, you can then grab the notepad and immediately write down everything you hear before it slips away.

It is obvious that the pigeons outside my window are speaking English. They must have been listening carefully to their human neighbours, and have managed to learn some useful phrases. The annoying thing is that they tend to repeat the same ones over and over again, so that you want to plead with them to shut up. Nevertheless, it is fascinating to try and identify what they are saying, and so learn something about pigeon social chit-chat.

There must be at least four birds that regularly meet in my garden, because they address each other by name. They are called: Freddie, Suzie, Julie, and Judy. These monikers must be quite common among the pigeon fraternity, as I have also heard them used in other parts of the country. Maybe you have too, and perhaps the conversations you have overheard were something like the one that took place outside my window this morning.

I managed to jot it down as it went along. Every word in this dialogue really was spoken by the birds themselves, I promise you. Here is the transcript. Try reading it aloud with a voice that you have heard pigeons use.

It commenced with the one who clearly thought of himself as the king pin of the little group: "It's Freddie, its Freddie, it's Freddie." He always seemed to have a lot to say for himself, and continued, "What ails you Suzie?"

"I'm alright, Freddie", was the response. But she then added, "This place is dirty." In order to emphasise the point, Suzie continued, "You're dirty, you're dirty, you're dirty."

Freddie was obviously not expecting such an affront to his dignity but, before he could respond, another voice piped up, "You're dirty, Suzie; you're dirty, Suzie."

"What's it got to do with you, Julie?" came the reply. Ah, so it seems that Julie must be Freddie's lady-friend, and she had lost no time in showing which side she was on.

No doubt bolstered by this show of support, Freddie chirped back at his antagonist, "What's the grumble, misery guts?"

"Look around you, it's everywhere", said Suzie.

Realising that she was probably right, but reluctant to admit it, Freddie's response was limited to a rather weak, "You're very, very, bossy; very, very bossy." And with that little barb, there was a short lull in the conversation.

The fourth member of the group must have then made an appearance. "Where's our tea, Judy?", one of the others asked.

"It's ready, it's ready", she replied, rather impatiently.

Not sure if he wanted any tea at this early hour, he was nevertheless urged on by his sparing partner. "It's time to try it, Freddie; it's time to try it."

Obediently, and in order to keep the peace, he presumably did so, but then felt obliged to exclaim: "It's cold, Suzie! It's cold Suzie"

Maybe Suzie was aware of this, but she missed no opportunity to play little tricks on Freddie because of his lack of attention to personal cleanliness. It also seemed that she and Judy were used to collaborating in the points-scoring game. "We're still a team, Suzie, we're still a team," her friend commented.

It appeared that this morning's encounter was coming to an end. "Let's go home soon, Suzie", Judy said. Seemingly her friend had not taken the hint, so Judy said with more urgency, "Let's get out of here, Suzie." This must have done the trick, as nothing more was heard from these two during the rest of the morning.

This just left the courting couple chatting in my garden. The sound of a barking dog broke the temporary silence. "Which doggie, which doggie?" Julie asked, and then added, "Let's go to it, Freddie, let's go to it."

"It's bigger than you, Julie", Freddie warned.

It seemed that Freddie had successfully dissuaded his lady friend from trying to initiate a confrontation with the local canine. But presumably still seeking some adventure, Julie asked her partner, "Where to now, Freddie"?

There was another pause, as if her boyfriend was trying to think of a suitable place to go. He started to say, "It's far too early, it's . . . . ."

Realising that no brilliant ideas were about to burst forth from his beak, Julie interrupted him and said, "Let's go now, Freddie."

And with that, they flew out of my garden. Silence prevailed. Oh dear, it's time for me to get up. No doubt the pigeons will be back again tomorrow.

Chapter 3

Humour therapy

It's a funny thing, humour. This is the title of a book by Anthony Chapman and Hugh Foot (Oxford: Pergamon, 1977). I just wish I had thought of it first, as it playfully and succinctly tells us a lot about the ability to see the funny side of life.

So then, why do we laugh; why do we utter those short bursts of noise that can range from low ruffs to high-pitched shrieks? How did it originate? Does it have any survival value for our species? Answers to these and similar questions will be suggested shortly, but here is a clue: "Being cheerful keeps you healthy. It is slow death to be gloomy all the time." Whom do you think uttered these wise words?

If you know they were written about one thousand years before the Christian Era, does that help? They are attributed to King Solomon, and the quotation is taken from a modern translation of Proverbs, chapter 17, verse 22. What they tell us is that, even in those ancient times, it was recognised that there was a link between personal disposition, or mood, and physical health. Some three thousand years later, boffins gave this a fancy name: 'psychoneuroimmunology'. This simply means that our mood affects our brain, the brain influences our immune system, and the immune system protects us from disease. Quite a brilliant observation by King Sol, don't you think?

Enough of Bible punching and long words. How far can we go back to discover the first signs of humour? Perhaps we should start with Hippocrates, the founder of modern medicine, who lived about four hundred years before the Christian Era. He said that our health is influenced by four bodily fluids: black bile, yellow bile, blood, and phlegm.

If this rather nauseous revelation has not already caused you to cast this story aside, and wonder if you can face your next meal, let it be quickly added that he called these fluids 'humours'. Hippocrates believed that you become ill if there is an imbalance between them, and that the physician's job was to restore the balance, or homeostasis as the medics might call it now. An old-fashioned form of greeting was to ask a person, "Are you in good humour?" If your humours were balanced, then you healthy and felt good.

Jokes have been around for a long time. Although there is some disagreement

about which was the earliest of these amusing little stories, a strong candidate originates from an inscription found in an Egyptian tomb completed in 2,600 BCE. This belonged to Pharaoh Sneferu, the father of Cheops who built the great pyramid at Giza. When the archaeologists were excavating the burial chamber, they realised that some of the hieroglyphics on the wall were in the form of a riddle. This question and answer format is still often used for jokes. A corny example is:

Question: "How do you get four elephants in a mini car?"

Answer: "Two in the front and two in the back!"

The Egyptian example loses a lot in translation, and is unlikely to raise a laugh these days, but here goes:

Question: "How do you entertain a bored pharaoh?"

"Answer: You sail a boatload of young women dressed only in fishing nets down the Nile, and urge the pharaoh to catch a fish!"

Whilst this is not very funny, it reveals much about Pharaoh Sneferu. One of the useful things about humour is that it can be used to criticise someone, especially a person in power. In medieval times, court jesters had license to poke fun at their king, provided that it was done in such a way that caused laughter – including by the butt of the joke himself. If anybody else tried this, it would likely be a case of: "Off with his head!"

Now Sneferu obviously had an eye for pretty young maidens. Nobody dare write about this whilst the pharaoh was alive, but one cheeky scribe decided to make sure that knowledge of his boss's extra-curricular dalliances was preserved for posterity. If he had been taken to task for doing this, he could simply have claimed that he was just having a joke.

Try maintaining the format of this riddle, but change the details to reflect the scandal involving any politician or other prominent person who has been in the news recently. You might find that you have created a topical joke that generates genuine laughter. This is what professional comedians do. They often just recycle or update old jokes, keeping the same framework but reflecting current issues.

Returning now to the history lesson, so far we have gone back in time via Hippocrates (400 BCE), Solomon (950 BCE), and Sneferu (2,600 BCE). Can we improve on this? Yes, we can, but it is to a time long before anything was written down. Some anthropologists believe that laughter originated as a 'roar of triumph', emitted by the victor in an ancient jungle duel. This was both a way of celebrating victory (just as over-enthusiastic sportspeople often do these days), and a communication to the world that you were the superior one, not to be meddled with. It was also a signal to those who might have been hiding from the danger that it was now safe for them to come out.

So, is the smile half way toward a laugh? No, it is quite the opposite. It developed from an expression of submission and appeasement by the loser, to acknowledge that your opponent had won, and that you were no longer a threat to him or her. Does this sound far-fetched? Well, what are you signifying when you meet someone in the street and smile at them? You are showing that you do not pose a risk, that you want to be friendly, and that you are pleased to see them.

Just two more definitions, to complete the picture. The earliest recorded comedy performances were ancient spring and fertility rites. In those days, a community's very survival depended heavily on the cycle of crop growing and animal breeding being successfully repeated each year. To help ensure that

Mother Nature would not let them down, plays were performed that depicted 'out with the old and in with the new'. These enactments were often obscene and debauched, so censorship was obviously as weak then as it often is in the theatre today.

Finally, we come to humour itself. This does not denote an action, something that one 'does', but it describes a 'disposition', a personality trait, a way of looking at life. Humour is all around us; we only have to open our eyes and observe it, just as an artist can see beauty in even mundane, everyday objects. Who would have thought that a painting of a bed or chair would make a good picture, but Vincent Van Gough certainly did. Think of the comedians who make us laugh the most. Is this because they tell complicated jokes? No, often it is because they just observe simple aspects of everyday life, and then add little twists or exaggerations to expose the humour that lies beneath.

In order for it to have originated in the first place, and survived for millennia, humour must contribute something to the survival of our species. It is, in fact, a defence mechanism; it helps us to cope with an ambiguous, often unjust world. Our powers of reasoning and logic cannot always explain or resolve the misfortunes in life that inevitably happen to us from time to time. One of the things that keep people going is an inherent belief that the world is basically a just place to be in. When this faith is shaken, we risk becoming so stressed that the usual coping mechanisms fail and a nervous breakdown might quickly follow.

But humankind has evolved a way of coming to terms with such experiences, even if they cannot be explained. The key word is 'creativity'. Unlike logic and reasoning, which predominantly use the left side of the brain, humour harnesses the power of creativity, which is mostly a right-brain activity. It requires the ability to see more than one possible cause for an event, or meaning of a statement and, along with them, a range of possible solutions.

Let us now apply this principle to problems we may encounter in life. Take for example a difficult personal relationship, or trouble at work. It is all too easy, and often wrong, to lay all the blame purely on oneself, or even the other person. Instead, we should ask ourselves: Why did it happen? How many factors were involved? What are the alternative courses of action we can take?

Note carefully the use of plurals in these questions. Once a person can see a range of causes and a variety of solutions, then he or she is back in the driving seat and in control of his or her life. The individual will now start to feel calmer and more objective about what may have happened, and what can be done about it.

Humour helps in yet another way. It encourages us to stop, step back, and try to put what initially seemed to be a traumatic situation in perspective. Were we perhaps being a touch over-dramatic? How really desperate was the situation? Was it the bitter end, or can we learn from this and resolve to carry on? Maybe, we can even start to see the funny side of what, at first, seemed to be a serious matter.

How does creativity relate to humour? Consider how we react to the punch-line of a joke. The first part of the story leads us in one direction, but then the ending appears to point us in a different one. It seems to be illogical, so our mind races through alternative explanations. Eventually we recognise one that does resolve the anomaly, but in an unexpected or novel way. We have used creativity to come to this conclusion, not reasoning, just like the way we can deal with personal problems. Here is a corny old joke that illustrates this process:

Parent phones the doctor: "Doctor, come quickly, our baby has swallowed a pen."

Doctor: "I'll be right over. What are you doing in the meantime?"

Parent: "Using a pencil."

This example, selected for its format, rather than its ability to generate unbridled hilarity, clearly demonstrates the mixture of logic and illogic that is unique to witticisms of this nature. For those people with no sense of humour at all, the story is sensible: well, what can you do if you lose your pen? You can use a pencil. Whilst the parent gave a logical response, it was not a socially acceptable one – we know that the welfare of the baby comes first, and this was the reason for the doctor's question.

Our brain becomes tense in its effort to understand the meaning of the parent's unexpected answer. When it has succeeded in solving the riddle, this tension is released through laughter. To obtain the maximum level of chortling, the time that this convoluted mental process takes should be about seven tenths of a second. If it is shorter, the effort will be too easy and the tension will not build; if it takes longer, then the tension starts to reduce spontaneously. Maybe knowing this gives us a new respect for the comedians who spend so much time honing their skills to give us a laugh.

Many people will say that they are not creative, and that they cannot tell jokes. Although this may not be strictly true, it is easy to boost your sense of humour and oil the creaking parts of the right side of the brain that may have been neglected. The simple answer is to avail yourself of some self-administered humour therapy. Still confused? Then this is what you do. Start a humour collection today.

You will need a scrapbook, and either a cupboard, drawer or box in which to store all your materials. Cut out from magazines or newspapers every cartoon that makes you laugh, and stick them in the album. Make a note of jokes before they slip your mind. Add any video, film, disk, audio tape and book that you have found to be funny. In fact, include anything in your collection that gives you a chuckle, in any medium. When you are feeling down or depressed, when nothing seems to be going well, turn to your humour store and spend as long as you can browsing through the items there.

It is impossible for misery and cheerfulness to exist together so, if you can raise a smile, then it surprising how quickly the spirits also start to rise. 'Perhaps I have been taking this too seriously', you may say to yourself; 'it was not so serious after all.' Just a word of caution, though. If you have had a serious problem, such as the loss of a loved one or a serious illness, or there has been a national tragedy, it is of course not appropriate to immediately reach for your joke collection. However, once you have come to terms with the trauma and are on your way to recovery, then humour has been proven to speed the healing process.

Proven? You may ask. Yes, proven, and here is the evidence. Firstly, laughing stimulates and then relaxes various muscles, helping to relieve conditions such as rheumatism and arthritis. Then it exercises the cardiac muscles, and this may decrease vulnerability to coronary heart disease. It clears residual air from the lungs and enhances oxygenation of the blood. Not only that, but a good laugh prompts the release of three types of hormone: catecholamine – this enhances alertness and reduces inflammation; endorphins – raises the spirits, helps control pain, and boosts the immune system; and immoglobulin-'A' – this protects us against upper-respiratory tract infections. There is certainly truth in the old maxim: 'laughter is the best medicine.'

Are you convinced yet? These are just the physical benefits of laughter, but the psychological ones are even more important. Rather than use my own words to support this statement, I defer to those uttered by the great Sigmund Freud. He did a lot of research on the benefits of jocularity, and wrote: "Humour takes its place in the great series of methods devised by man for evading the compulsion to suffer." On another occasion he said: "The world is child's play, the very thing to jest about."

Are you convinced now? Then don't sit around reading this book, make a start on your own humour collection right away. Follow the advice of that perceptive King Solomon who, three thousand years ago, wrote "Being cheerful keeps you healthy." It was true then, and it is true now.

Chapter 4

What people did in 1868

Funny how we remember odd things from our childhood. One of mine was looking through the situations vacant columns in a local newspaper in the Yorkshire woollen town where the family lived, and seeing advertisements for a 'Left hand twister-in'. This would have been in the early nineteen-fifties, and the job would have been one of the specialist trades in the local textile mills. It was a mystery then what this work entailed, and it is still a mystery to me now. Thus, it was time to do some investigating.

A search on the World Wide Web eventually revealed that a 'twister-in' was:

"A textile worker who twists or ties new warp threads onto ends left in the harness." However, there was no mention of what the left-hand version of this task was, or indeed if there was also a right-hand companion. When I contacted the editor of same local paper I read as a youngster, he kindly published my message on the letters page to see if anyone could solve this mystery. No response has been received as I start to write this piece but, if an answer is forthcoming, I shall share it with you later.

However, this is not the only textile job with an unusual name. You could also be employed as a 'Drawboy' (weaver's assistant), 'Scribbler' (in a Scribbing Mill where wool was carded), 'Slubber Doffe' (remover of bobbins from the spindles), 'Stripper' (no, not the obvious, but one who removed the rubbish from carding machines) or 'Woollen Billy Piecer' (sounds painful, but was actually the piecing together the broken yarns), to name but a few.

If you thought these titles would look silly on your curriculum vitae, then maybe you would prefer to be a 'Greasy Percher'. This job involved throwing a length of woven cloth from the loom onto a 'Perch', and then inspecting it for faults. Because the woollen yarn still had a high lanolin content from the sheep's wool, it was greasy to the touch. The next stage in the processing was scouring the piece to remove the oils, after which it was it inspected again but this time on the Finisher's Perch.

The textile industry was not the only one that had jobs with intriguing titles. How many people today can describe themselves as a 'Saggar Maker's Bottom Knocker'? This job originated in the pottery manufacturing centres. Apparently, a 'Saggar' is a fireclay container used in a kiln. Making one was a skilled task, except for the base that just required clay being forced into a metal ring, with the aid of a mallet. A young boy often did this, and he was given perhaps the most memorable job title ever to appear in an occupational directory. No doubt this is all an automated process these days, thereby eliminating the cue for many a cheeky joke. Other fascinating occupations from the potteries include 'Batter Man', 'Clay Treader', 'Disintegrator Attendant', 'Flat Knocker', and 'Sliphouse Man'. The demise of such occupational names surely robs the English language of some of its richness.

My interest in jobs of yesteryear was renewed recently when clearing out some old documents. Among them was a facsimile of the very first issue of the advertising journal *Exchange and Mart* (now part of the Newsquest Media Group). This was published as a newssheet from 1868 until 2009, but now just operates as an internet resource. Whereas today it specialises in motor vehicles, in its earlier days it covered almost anything. The paper was divided into several sections.

The first was 'The Exchange' which, as the name suggests, comprised invitations to swap items. The cost of placing an advertisement was one old penny for ten words. Often the advertiser just stated "open to offers", but at other times was more specific. One wanted to swap a poodle for good jewellery; another offered a donkey for a basket carriage. A person obviously keen on music wrote: "I have a gentleman's gold pin, and four small French dancing dolls for a piano." An individual who presumably already had a musical instrument indicated that he or she had some dry water colour paints, and would like classical music in return. Another wished to exchange a concertina for a violin.

Some advertisers could expect a visit from the police if they today expressed a desire to exchange a large shower bath with force pump, and a light double-barrel gun, for a miniature billiard table. Likewise, another person owned a large five-barrelled revolver made by Lancaster, and wished to exchange it for a pocket-sized, breach-loading model. There is no mention of fire-arm licences, so presumably they were not required in those days.

Unsurprisingly, in view of its name, the second section of this publication was 'The Mart', and it contained a wide range of goods for sale. Maybe you would be looking to purchase some cows, especially ones freshly imported from Alderney and Guernsey, and delivered free by rail to any part of England. It would have been interesting to see what prices were being asked, but they were not included in either of the two advertisements for these animals. If something smaller was your need, a breeder was offering eggs, presumably fertilised, from his prize fowls for sitting at seven shillings and sixpence per dozen. This is equivalent to about forty pounds today (in 2017), and does seem rather expensive. His duck eggs were cheaper, being just five shillings a dozen (about twenty-five pounds).

If it was horses you wanted, you could buy a five-year old cob, at 13-hands and 2 inches, for twenty-eight guineas (£3,116), or a 16-hands bay gelding for one hundred and fifty guineas (£16,695). However, a pair of Galloways, 15-hands, would cost you two hundred and twenty guineas (£23,330). These prices are certainly not cheap. Horses are currently being advertised from about a thousand pounds upwards, although you can expect to pay from five to ten thousand for a decent pony.

Perhaps you were looking for specific books. If so, you could not go far wrong by agreeing to purchase Wright's *History of Domestic Manners in England under the Anglo-Saxons*, first published in 1862. It would cost you just seven shillings then, equivalent to thirty-seven pounds today. Copies still exist, and the text can now be viewed on-line. If your preference was for sport, you could buy one hundred volumes of *Sporting Magazine*, which were stated to be "Full of curious plates and prize ring contests." It would cost you seven pounds and ten shillings then, now equivalent to a whopping seven hundred and ninety-five pounds.

The third section in this first edition of *Exchange and Mart* brings us back to the topic of what people did for a living back then. It is devoted to jobs, firstly listing 'Wants' and then 'Vacancies'. The cost of placing these advertisements is stated as 'one postage stamp for every four words.' Although the value of the stamp is not stated, the penny post was still in operation in those days, provided the letter did not weigh more than one ounce. The postings provide an illuminating snapshot of the times, especially concerning domestic employment.

There are just over one hundred entries from people looking for work – sixty per cent being by women, but only twelve advertised vacancies, which suggests there may have been a high level of unemployment. The greatest number of 'wants' was for housemaids (fifteen), followed by eleven for cooks, and seven each for ladies maids, grooms, and coachmen. In many cases, the maid seeking work stated her age, with the youngest being only sixteen, and the rest all in their twenties. Most specifically mentioned how many years of character references they had. Two were applicants for what was presumably the more senior job of housekeeper, and they declared their ages to be in the mid-forties.

Rather intriguingly, several maids specified wanting a position where a footman or other male is kept. Could this be for protection, or to ensure that help was available for any heavy lifting, or even a possible romance? Unfortunately, the advertisers are no longer available to ask. The posting by the youngest hints at the difficulties many experienced in those days. It reads: "Housemaid, under, or to make herself generally

useful. From the country, age 16. Good references."
Does the latter mean she already had work experience,
or just that acquaintances had provided her with
character references to help her obtain her first job?
Sadly, child labour at that time was the norm rather
than the exception.

What about the men seeking employment?
Coachmen and grooms made up the largest category,
reflecting the reliance at that time on horse transport.
Two of the advertisers were aged only nineteen, and
one, who was twenty-one, said that he had nine years
good character. Does this imply that he was working
from the age of twelve? In contrast, another who gave
his age as forty-three, mentioned that he had just two
years of good character, and was married with no
family. What was he doing in his earlier working life?
Did he have an unfortunate experience that made him
seek pastures new? How interesting it would be to
interview these people now. It would not be surprising
to learn that many of them might have tales of real
hardship to relate.

The majority of those in this horse-related category
specified that they could drive a pair, which implies
more skill than just handling one horse at a time. Some

men must have been desperate for work, as one stated that he could also wait at the table, another that he would have no objection to making himself generally useful, whilst a third added gardening to his list of can dos. One young man said that he had no objection to going abroad.

Other jobs for males included footman, butler, and gardener. One applicant for the latter was the only one among either the men or the women who stated what he was earning in his last job. It was twenty-four shillings a week – equivalent to one hundred and sixty pounds in today's money.

It is noticeable that all the people seeking employment, whether male or female, were looking for domestic service. The few advertisements posted by employers looking for workers contained vacancies for only three such positions. One of these was for a general servant, and the wages offered were twelve pounds all found. If this was the annual rate, it would be the equivalent of just less than twenty-five pounds per week today. Another was for a cook, with a more generous wage of thirty pounds (over sixty pounds per week now).

One of the vacancies that were not for domestic staff comprised managers for the meat, grocery, and cheesemongery departments at the emporium of the Housekeepers Association, Limited. Another wanted applicants for an office keeper to take charge of city offices. There was one for a warehouseman, and another for a traveller for druggists' sundries goods. None of these quoted a salary. Finally, there was one for a nurse, not in a hospital but for looking after children in a private home. The remuneration offered for this was sixteen pounds all found (nearly thirty-three pounds per week today).

What a difference one hundred and fifty years makes! Although a few royal palaces and stately homes will still require servants, only a miniscule percentage of the population will find employment in this capacity now. There was no social security or unemployment benefits in the eighteen-hundreds, and the divide between the rich and poor was wide. Many people were only minimally educated, and had to rely on domestic service with the landed gentry and other wealthy citizens; they would surely starve if they could not find employment.

Although not included in this first edition of
Exchange and Mart, jobs in the trades, crafts, building,
and manufacturing sectors, as well as food production,
retailing and distribution, would still have been required
in the old days. Likewise would be those in the
professions such as education, banking, medicine and
the law. The army and navy would require recruits, but
the birth of the air force was still a thing of the future.
However, there were no motor vehicles, no computers,
and the generation of electric power was only at the
experimental stage. The range and numbers of carers
and social workers was much more limited then than it
is now, unless you were rich and could afford to
employ one.

A glance at the situations vacant columns today
reveals a very wide range of opportunities. Cleaners
other domestic staff are still advertised for, but many
positions that would have previously been for domestic
help in privileged homes, are instead now required in
the much expanded hotel and catering industries.
Groomsmen and coach drivers, at least for the horse
drawn variety, no longer feature highly in the lists of
vacancies.

Jobs now abound in information technology, logistics, the media, and science.

Current occupations in manufacturing embrace diverse and often highly technical skills. Transport has expanded to include aircraft as well as advanced road and rail vehicles. Schools and universities require many more teachers than was previously the case, in order to help prepare people for work in this technological age. Many more employees are required for health care, and these jobs also need higher levels of skills than was the case many years ago.

Yes, the opportunities to embark on a satisfying career of your choice are now almost boundless and, if you are out of work, you can expect financial help. Do we still yearn for the 'good old days'? Perhaps we should be grateful for the advances that have taken place, and are ongoing, and ensure that they are not abused. Thank you *Exchange and Mart* for reminding us what working life was like one hundred and fifty years ago.

Post script: So what about the 'Left-handed twister-in' that sparked off this enquiry into jobs of yesteryear? Three replies to my letter posted in the local newspaper were eventually received. One was kindly submitted by a Mr Raymond Ellis, who is a trustee of Colne Valley Museum in Golcar, Huddersfield. He wrote that 'Twisters in' could either be left- or right-handed. Although most people are naturally right-handed, a sizeable minority are left-handed. If you employ one of each, you can start with two people in the centre of a warp and work outwards in both directions at the same time; the job is then completed in half the time. So there we have it, mystery now solved!

Chapter 5

The meaning of dreams

Do you dream at night? If so, do you remember what you dreamt about? It may be surprising but, apart from rare cases of neurological impairment, everybody does dream. If you did not have them, then you probably wouldn't be sitting down reading this story. Assuming you had survived in your dreamless existence, then the psychiatric ward of a hospital would likely be your home now. Does this sound a tad over-dramatic? Supporting evidence will be presented shortly, but first here is a bit of background.

Dreams have been mentioned in writings since the beginning of recorded history. A Greek author called Antiphon wrote a book about them in the fourth century before the Christian Era, and Egyptian scripts date back to about two thousand years BCE, Several dreams are reported in the Hebrew Scriptures, including in Daniel (4:5-27) where the prophet interpreted one that King Nebuchadnezzar had, correctly predicting the monarch's seven years of madness. In Genesis (41:1-32), we read that Joseph deciphered the Pharaoh's dream that foretold of seven years of plenty followed by a similar period of famine.

These two biblical examples are particularly interesting because it appears that the dreams correctly foretold of future events. Indeed, many ancient cultures, and even some individuals today, believe that the images and messages come from an outside source, and are communications from the gods, or from people they knew who had died. Whilst this is not the generally held scientific view, we can never be sure of these things. Thus, the views of those who like to think that dreams have a divine origin, or are messages from departed loved ones, must be respected. The topic of dreams predicting future events is another one that will be discussed later in this essay.

If you cannot remember the content of the dreams that you most certainly have had, you are not alone. Only about fifty-five per cent of people can recall them and, even then, only sometimes. In the year nineteen fifty-three, it was discovered that, several times during the night, our eyes make rapid movements behind closed lids. When people were woken up during these episodes, they usually stated that they had been dreaming. This was only rarely the case at other times during the night. Thus, researchers now had a simple way of measuring what happens during a typical period of sleep.

For about the first ninety minutes of sleep, we descend into a deep, relaxed and dreamless state. Then we ascend to a more mentally active level where this 'rapid eye movement' (REM), and most dreams, occur. This first occurrence lasts about ten minutes, after which we descend again to a deeper, dreamless, level. This cycle of ascent and descent is repeated from four to seven times during the night, with the dreaming periods increasing in duration to about forty minutes. In total, we dream for an average of approximately two of the eight hours typically spent sleeping.

Some significant changes occur in the brain during these episodes. The parts concerned with logic and critical judgement are turned off. This means that we do not block or censor any thoughts or ideas that are generated, as we sometimes subconsciously do when we are awake. The ability to perform physical actions is also shut down, and our muscles remain relaxed. This is believed to be a safety mechanism that prevents us from trying to act out our dreams and possibly injuring either ourselves, or anyone near us. The resulting 'sleep paralysis', as it is known, can manifest itself in our dreams as a frightening sensation of not being able to run, swim or shout when there is danger.

In addition, the parts of the brain responsible for imagery, vision, creativity, and the emotions remain active, and we are motivated to search for answers that have eluded us during our waking hours. All of these neurological changes have a significant effect on our dream content. Surprisingly, with sufficient practice and patience, we can manipulate this altered state so that dreams can become very useful – another resource to help us cope with life. Does this sound too much like science fiction? Well, please read on and judge for yourself.

Before we deal with this aspect, however, a few other points need to be covered. Firstly, here is a warning about dream deprivation. Dreaming is very important, as it allows emotional feelings to be dissipated, and memories to be either consolidated and stored, or discarded as no longer needed. Deliberately preventing someone dreaming by waking them up each time REM is seen, will stop these essential psychological processes occurring, and also cause chronic tiredness and fatigue. If prolonged, the individual will be unable to function normally, and will ultimately suffer a complete mental breakdown. Do you still think that you are one of those who never dream?

Many people have wondered where the thoughts and images in their dreams come from, and there are several theories. In the year eighteen hundred and ninety-nine, Sigmund Freud published his book *The Interpretation of Dreams*. In it, he stated that our more primitive and animalistic impulses and desires – often sexual or aggressive – remain hidden in the unconscious, being held down by the conscious mind. In our dreams, this control relaxes, allowing us to play out our often socially unacceptable urges and wishes. However, the images and content have been altered and cannot be taken at face value; they have to be interpreted by an expert in order to uncover their underlying urges and anxieties. He called dreams 'the royal road to the unconscious mind' and used them in his psychotherapy.

Carl Jung, who for a time worked with Freud, had an idea that is literally mind-blowing. He thought that dreams tap into a 'collective unconscious', a vast reservoir or spirit world of archetypal symbols. These have been inherited from the previous experiences of all humanity that has ever lived. It is these symbols that populate our dreams. To delve further into Jung's ideas would take up far too many pages of this book, so interested readers may wish to consult more specialised publications.

Fortunately, the other theories to be mentioned are more straight-forward. The third idea, Championed by Fritz Pearls, is known as 'reflecting our concerns'. It maintains that, whilst we are sleeping, the brain is processing information of which it has yet to make sense. The dreams replay events, especially those that are emotional such as worries, concerns and unresolved issues. When we have a traumatic experience, during the daytime we are preoccupied with dealing with the practicalities of what happened. This leaves little opportunity for the emotional aspect to be accepted and resolved, so our dreams help us to come to terms with this important process. Indeed, research has shown that at least three-quarters of dreams are on negative topics; cheerful ones are much rarer.

Moving on to theory number four, Finnish neuroscientist Antti Revonsuo suggested that dreaming developed thousands of years ago as an evolutionary strategy. Primitive humans lived in a physically hostile world, and faced many dangers and threats from invading tribes and wild animals. If the only opportunities to learn how to successfully defend themselves occurred when the events actually happened, then many lives would likely be lost before the necessary skills had been mastered. Revonsuo's idea is that, whilst we are sleeping, the brain simulates threatening events so that we can recognise the danger, and practise defensive strategies within the safety of our dreams. Even today, sports psychologists use 'imagining techniques' to help people rehearse for an important event, by successfully leading them through it in their imaginations.

The fifth suggestion is very simple: the brain needs to keep busy and entertained whilst we are asleep. It does this by replaying 'home-made B-movies', so the images come from real or fantasised episodes from our own lives. Equally straight-forward is the last theory, which is known as 'Garbage'. We absorb a lot of images and detail during the day. When we are asleep, our brain sifts through all this material and files anything useful in long-term memory. What remains is just dumped into garbage, and lost, thus preventing our little grey cells from being overloaded. Our dream images represent these thoughts and mental pictures as they are being erased or filed.

Which of these ideas appeal to you, if any? Maybe each of them has something to offer. What most of the theories have in common is that they identify dreams as playing a useful role in our lives. Could one of these uses be that they can foretell the future, just like the two biblical examples did? Some reported examples include American President Abraham Lincoln predicting his own death, two weeks before he was assassinated by John Wilkes Booth in eighteen sixty-five. Then, when Henry Morton Stanley was in Africa trying to find David Livingstone, he dreamt about the death of a relative, and this turned out to be true.

Author Mark Twain dreamt that he saw his brother's corpse in a coffin, a few weeks before the brother died, and Charles Dickens said he had a dream about a woman called Miss Napier, who was dressed in red, shortly before being visited by such a person.

Whilst these may seem amazing, the most outstanding example concerns an Irish peer named Lord Kilbracken, who is said to have dreamt the winners of nine horse races within a short period of time. Born as

John Godley in London in nineteen-twenty, he lived to
be eighty-five years old. He went to Oxford where, for
a time, he claimed he could predict the winners,
including that of a Grand National race where the horse
came in at the odds of eighteen to one. A remarkable
ability that most of us would wish to share. However, a
later report stated that Godley's talent proved only
temporary.

Do any of these cases support the notion that dreams
really can predict the future? Sadly, this is very
unlikely. In the case of the racing winners, professional
gamblers are skilled at reading all the signs, and can
often show a profit – at least for a time. With the other
examples, there are doubts as to the accuracy of the
reporting, and the likelihood that clues were present,
such as knowing that a relative was ill and death would
not be far away. Nevertheless, it would be unfair to
completely shut the door on this; if you have had an
example of prediction that was convincing, then the
ability of dreams to do this is real for you.

We are on stronger ground if we now turn to
problem-solving and creativity – one of the reasons
why dreams really are useful to us. We have all
probably used the expression 'sleep on it' when we

have been able to come to a decision. In the morning we may have wakened with the answer – a 'Eureka', or 'Ah ha' moment.

It has been reported that Samuel Taylor Coleridge dreamt his poem *Kubla Khan* word for word, and that Richard Wagner dreamt his opera *Tristan and Isolde*. Likewise, it is claimed that the plot of *Frankenstein* came to Mary Shelly in dream, and that of *Doctor Jekyll and Mister Hyde* entered Robert Louis Stevenson's mind in the same way. Other examples include Paul McCartney claiming that he dreamt the tune of his song *Yesterday*, and that the inspiration for the Theory of Relativity came to Albert Einstein in a dream.

Were these and other cases messages from the 'outside' that would otherwise never have materialised? Psychologists have investigated claims that dreams have generated novel solutions. Their conclusion is that, in each case, the person involved was already an expert in his or her field, and had been working hard on the issue in question. Remember that logic, critical judgement, and the 'cognitive censor' are all turned off when we dream, but that the motivation to seek answers is very much active.

Thus, whilst the 'expert' was sleeping and dreaming, conscious control of his or her thoughts was relaxed. The solution that was being held back during the waking hours was then free to emerge during the dream, and was transferred to long-term memory. When that person woke up, the dream was probably forgotten but the longed-for answer suddenly appeared. A very useful skill if we could learn to do it. And we can. There is an amusing little rule of thumb that a physicist once reported. He said, "I look at a problem with my front brain, think about it with my middle brain, and then put it to my back (unconscious) brain to solve itself." Difficult to do literally, but the idea behind letting the brain work unhindered is certainly sound.

If you want to train yourself to be able to make full use of your dreams to solve problems and help with life coping, here is what you do. Obviously, you must be able to remember your dreams, and we know that only just over half of the population can. Firstly, just before you go to sleep, use auto-suggestion to tell yourself that you *will* remember your dreams. Repeat this as many times as you can. Secondly, keep a writing pad or voice recorder next to your bed. Dream memories rapidly fade, so note down what you can remember, whether it makes sense or not, immediately on waking. Thirdly, if there is an issue that you specifically wish to resolve, write it down on a piece of paper and focus on it as you drift off to sleep.

Being able to succeed in all this is no easy task, and only about half the people who try this manage to do so. As with many aspects of life, perseverance is needed for success. Apart from waking up with the answers to your questions, you may find you can enter the world of 'lucid dreams'. In that state, you will know you are dreaming, but you will be able to control your dreams to a certain extent. Finally, keep a 'dream diary', and record in it both your main life events and concerns, and the content of your dreams. You can then see if there are any links between the two sets of data. Are your dreams trying to tell you something – warning you perhaps?

Many people claim to be able to interpret dreams, but often their explanations are not based on serious research. Investigations by psychologists and other specialists are carried out in sleep laboratories. They try to link dream content with everyday events, just like you can do. The images we see are mostly triggered by an emotion, and the brain then draws on random episodes from our lives to try and put together a coherent story based on this. The result is often silly or meaningless, so it is important to ignore the superficial details and instead try to identify the emotion that is running through the narrative. Maybe this reveals a worry that was being kept hidden in the unconscious, so that you can now recognise it and take the necessary action.

Researchers have found only a few reliable links between dreams and events, but here is a list of some of them to help you interpret your own dreams. All but the last two reflect negative emotions. However, remember that whatever you discover is not something to cause you extra worry, but it is a sign that you need to do something about it.

Slippery slope—failure to make progress (you need to change, or seek help)

Crossroads—a point of decision (which way to go?)

Packing for a holiday—a need to escape from everyday problems

Weapons that don't work— a sense of being powerless

House or room—this is you: what do you see? Do you wish to change it?

Clock or watch—your heart, the seat of your emotions. Is it fast, slow, or stopped?

Mirror—this is how you see yourself? Is it a strange reflection?

Unfamiliar surroundings—danger of overstepping self-knowledge

Failure to be understood—feeling of inadequacy

Falling—you have climbed too high, and now feel insecure

Being chased—need to face an aspect of yourself that is being denied

Missing a train or appointment—anger and frustration

Bright eyes—a healthy inner life

Light—an insight is about to happen

On the subject of nightmares, more common in children than adults, these are caused by stress, fear, emotional difficulties, and anxiety. In particular, they indicate a struggle for self-identity. The dream is telling the individual not to run away, but to turn and face the threat or demon, and find a way of dealing with it. If you suffer from nightmares, try to identify what is troubling you, and resolve it. The unpleasant dreams will then not reoccur. You can also help others to do this.

You now have sufficient information to start your own dream-interpretation practice, as well as use this very valuable tool as a resource for improving your own life. To finish with, here are two quotations to give you nightmares.

The first is from Martin Rees, the Astronomer Royal, heard on a television programme several years ago: "Are we dreaming *all* the time? It is just that when we are awake we are influenced by what we take in through the senses!"

The second is from a past President of the Royal Society: "Maybe we are just a computer simulation of inhabitants from another universe!"

Yes, good questions – how do you know you are not dreaming right now?

Makes you think, doesn't it!

Chapter 6

The seed

It is not often that one can become emotional about a seed. We are all soppy when it comes to baby people, and we just love puppies and even lion cubs. But seeds?

Now in retirement, one of my pleasures is growing tomatoes in the greenhouse. Mind you, we did not even have one of these glazed outbuildings until a few years ago, but a do-it-yourself kit was spotted in a catalogue. When it arrived, the assembly seemed very straight forward, something the instruction booklet said could be completed in a single eight-hour day. Well, double that time, add the help of a friend, sprinkle liberally with curses and broken fingernails, and there it was – my very own greenhouse!

Come the spring and, not wanting to bother with seeds, it was off to the nursery to buy six tomato plants with a mixture of varieties to yield early, main, and late crop fruits. The first attempt went well, and my wife and I both savoured the pleasure of eating home-grown produce, harvested straight from the vine. In due course, an oil heater and an automated irrigation system were installed, so that neither cold snaps nor summer holidays would jeopardise the growth-cycle of these food-yielding, botanical creations.

The next two or three seasons were equally productive, although there was no guarantee that the same tomato varieties would always be available at the nursery. Last year one of the plants produced an enormous, ribbed fruit. When fully ripe, it weighed exactly one kilogram – well over two pounds, was almost half a metre in circumference, and had a diameter of sixteen centimetres – more than six inches. Apart from three much smaller siblings, that was the total yield of this specimen, although it probably represented a similar combined weight of fruit to that produced by any of the other plants in the greenhouse.

After harvesting, this large tomato lasted us for several days, and was delicious. The edible flesh extended right to the middle. We resolved to grow this variety every year, so it was just a matter of checking on its name. Oh dear, there was no label on the container, but it was obviously one of the range of 'Beefsteaks'. Checking the photographs of examples of this group failed to identify specifically which one we had. There was only one option remaining – save some seeds from the tomatoes we had grown.

But our one kilogram wonder and its companions were so fleshy that none of these little germ cells were visible. Surely this noble plant was not destined to die barren, without leaving any progeny. Mother Nature cannot be so cruel. In a state of mild panic, the very heart of the large fruit was carefully scraped out and inspected for any sign of a seed. Eventually, a single tiny form, rather flat and little bigger than a pin head, was found. It was not certain that it was indeed what we were seeking; it might have been just a small piece of the tomato's core or skin. Even if this were a viable spore, could this species survive and propagate if it only produced a single miserable little seed per plant?

As this doubtful speck was all that could be found, it was reverently placed on a piece of tissue paper and left to dry. The paper was then popped into a small tin, which was left on a shelf during the winter months, and temporarily forgotten. The following year, in the early spring, the container was retrieved and the paper removed. With very little optimism, some compost was put in the tin, and the seed – if that is what it was – was pushed into it with a finger, and then covered with more soil. After sprinkling with some water, the little planter was placed on a windowsill. In the meantime, six new seedlings had been purchased and were installed in the greenhouse.

Nothing happened for a week or two, which just seemed to confirm that what was saved and planted was not actually a seed at all. But then, low and behold, one day a tiny green shoot appeared. It resembled a single strand of the type of cress that is grown in a cardboard box for salads and boiled egg sandwiches. There was little hope that this would actually be a tomato plant, but more likely a weed that had contaminated the soil. Still, it was worth letting it develop some more to see what it would become.

It was very slow growing, and continued to retain its weed-like appearance even when it did reach the height of a few centimetres. Eventually it was time to transfer it from its little tin into a plant pot, and place this in the greenhouse. So far no leaves had developed to help identify the growth, although it did continue to increase in size. At last, some side-shoots appeared on the stem. Could they be leaves of a tomato plant? Although still very tiny, their shape was carefully compared with those on this year's plants, which by now had almost reached their full height.

Well, yes, they were not simply smooth and lenticular, but had notches and lobes that punctuated their oval circumferences. Wow! If this was indeed a tomato plant, then our remarkable matriarch of last year did not die childless, but would live on through her daughter. It was difficult not to feel a sense of wonder. Had our specimen been singled-out by 'somebody up there' to be a survivor? Maybe it had a special mission to achieve before it too went to meet its maker.

This called for a celebration but first, in order to give this juvenile the best chance of growing big and strong, it was given its final house move into a larger pot. It did, however, look somewhat out of place; such a little thing competing for attention against its already mature and impressive neighbours.

Although it may have been a slow starter, our orphaned foster child – for that was what it had become to us, soon made up for lost time, and grew remarkably quickly. So impressive was its development that twice-daily height measurements were taken to check if our eyes were playing tricks. During a two-week period, the average daily growth was nearly four centimetres – one and a half inches. In early July, the growing tip was nipped off when it reached just over one hundred centimetres – nearly three and half feet. It then proudly stood shoulder to shoulder with its colleagues in the greenhouse.

As was the case last year, very few flowers were produced, and only four tomatoes. One looked set to develop into another monster, dwarfing its three siblings. Just like its mother, this offspring obviously knew just what size of family it could support.

But then – had disaster struck?

Just as everything seemed to be going so well, one day purple spots were seen developing on some of the leaves. Our brave little seed had defied the odds to survive and prosper thus far; was it all going to end prematurely due to a deadly disease? An urgent investigation of the symptoms suggested that the cause of these blemishes may have been a difficulty the plant was having absorbing water and nutrients. Apparently, the purple colour is due to a lack of phosphorus. The solution: maintain regular watering and feeding, and avoid excess heat or cold.

Intensive care was clearly needed. Like a dedicated nurse tending a patient, paying attention to this plant's every need, and carefully monitoring its progress, became almost an obsession. Transplanting into a larger pot would no doubt have helped it to obtain the nourishment it needed, but this would be too risky to try now. Because at the time there had been little hope that it would grow into the strapping adult that it had become, its last re-planting had not been into the biggest container available. Moving house at this stage could result in fatal damage. Please don't leave us now, brave plant; don't let this be the end of the line for your family tree, was our plea.

Next morning, before breakfast, the first thought was to see if our botanical invalid was showing any sign of recovery or, perish the thought, giving up its fight for survival. Mercifully, it did not look much different which, at least, gave some cause for optimism. The medical report would read: 'the patient is in a stable condition.' Although the purple spots were still there, the leaves were not curling up or dropping off. There was likewise little change after a further two days. Another day passed, and then: was it imagination, or did the blemishes look just a little less prominent than they had been earlier?

With continued nurturing, the plant survived and the four fruits continued to grow. The largest was not round but was shaped rather like a boat with a blunt prow and stern. On careful inspection, it looked like two of the original flowers may have fused together, and produced a pair of conjoined twins. Still, it would be as wrong to judge a tomato by its looks, as it is to judge a book by its proverbial cover, or the inner beauty of a person by his or her mug shot. The ultimate test of this ugly duckling would be its taste, and that would come later.

Happily, life continued without further incident until, in mid-September, the largest fruit had developed its ripe red colour, and was ready for harvesting. It had not reached the dimensions of its parent, but still weighed in at a healthy three hundred and fifty grams, which is over three quarters of a pound, and had a circumference of thirty-three centimetres – more than one foot. Now came the long-awaited moment: firstly, what did it taste like? Secondly, had it produced any seeds?

With some trepidation, the first slice was cut. Could that be a seed already? Three more slices and yes, several more were revealed. These were eagerly, but carefully, harvested, and transferred to a piece of kitchen paper to dry off in a safe place. And now for the taste; will it equal that of its noble parent, which had long departed to that vegetable garden in the sky? Again 'yes', it was delicious. Mission accomplished. Phew!

There were still the three other siblings in the process of ripening, one being rather oval in shape but the other two were round, if you can call something ribbed and knobbly 'round'. Thus, plenty of opportunity for further seeds, if needed. Now, with more confidence than a year ago, there is hope that these will germinate next season, and so produce the third generation. And, of course, it need not stop there.

As suggested by the opening sentence of this story, the whole episode aroused some unexpected emotions. There had been this lovely big tomato, and the desire to grow some more like it. Then the careful search for seeds that yielded just a single, doubtful candidate. Would this be the end of the mother plant, who gave her life so that we could enjoy her fruits, but whose apparent barrenness meant that she would not leave any descendents to follow in her footsteps?

But this one little ovum was a fighter, a survivor that was destined to succeed against all the odds. If it had not been found and nurtured, its family line would have come to an ignominious end. With no intention of failure, it had valiantly tolerated the rather casual care-giving it had received, especially in its early life, before proudly blossoming into the fine specimen of which its mother would be proud. Well done, little fellow, we salute your perseverance.

Rest assured that we shall do all that we can to see that your lineage survives and prospers; it is nothing less than you deserve.

<u>Post script</u>: It is now late May the following year. So far only one of the seeds saved from last year is showing possible signs of germinating. Are we going to be blessed with any grandchildren?

Chapter 7

The meaning of life

Probably the most profound questions that a person can ask are: Where do we come from? What is the meaning of life? Is there a life hereafter? The answers to each of these will depend very much on whether or not the individual is religious and, if they are, which religion they follow. Although those with a faith will likely find the questions easier to answer than will those who are atheists or agnostics, the aim of this essay is not to preach, but to try and address the issues from all sides. There can be no definitive answers; the questions are just too big and have taxed the greatest minds, but there should be no harm in trying to make a few suggestions.

The third question, that concerning what happens when we shed this mortal coil, will be saved for another chapter of this book, so let us turn to the first question: where do we come from? Religion and science are not too far apart on certain fundamental aspects of how it all started. The cosmologists' 'Big Bang Theory' on the origin of the universe does not necessarily disagree with the beliefs of the creationists. In particular, the order that various elements of the land, sea, and then the living plants and animals came along, are similar.

However, the human mind has great difficulty trying to comprehend aspects such as infinity, before time began, and what sparked the whole of creation. If there was just an empty void, we struggle to understand how something could have been created out of nothing. Logic tells us that, if there really was a time when there was absolutely

nothing, then there would still be nothing now.

In my book *What do we Know About God?* I mentioned that, for those who have a religious faith, the opening verses of both Genesis ("In the beginning, God created the heavens and the earth") and John's Gospel ("In the beginning was the Word . . . and the Word was God") do at least provide an answer. As regards the question of where God, if there is one, came from, one just has to accept that the deity was always there; there can be no other explanation.

The secular equivalent would be that there was in the beginning just energy, without form. According to Albert Einstein's famous theory, energy can be transformed into matter, and matter can be transformed into energy ($E = MC^2$). Thus, it could be that originally there was just invisible energy (could this be what God actually is?). Then we had 'The Big Bang', when this primordial force, or at least some of it, was converted into matter and the universe was born. The laws of physics, chemistry and biology then worked their magic until, nearly fourteen billion years later, human beings were either created or evolved, depending on your point of view about our origins.

The Hasidic Jewish tradition embraces a particularly appealing notion of the why, as well as the how, of creation. It is known as 'Contraction', or 'Tzimtzum' theory. There was a time when only God existed, and he (assuming the masculine) existed everywhere. Being all-powerful, he had no needs, but he was morally benevolent and wanted to share his goodness with others. Because he was omnipresent, he had to contract in order to make space for his creative light to shine. This then became the primordial dynamic of creation – he shared his goodness by creating the world. But he did not just leave it at that; he remains with each and every one of us whilst, paradoxically, granting us free will.

Time now to have a look at the second big issue: the meaning of life. Other ways of putting this are: Is there a reason we are here? Does our life have any purpose? Do we have a mission that we are expected to fulfil? If we ask such questions of a random sample of people, as mentioned above the suggested answers are likely to be heavily influenced by religious beliefs. This issue will now be examined from both viewpoints, starting with the secular ideas, although many of these might also be embraced by those with a faith.

Mission statements issued by atheist and Humanist organisations will be considered shortly. Firstly, however, comments from people who were presumably considered worthy enough to have their words immortalised, were examined to see if any meaningful patterns emerged. There are probably thousands of such offerings, but a fairly cursory search unearthed over sixty-five of them. A quarter of them were based on the notion that there is no universal meaning to life, but that we each create our own. Each person needs to discover what is special to him or her; what it is that we make of ourselves during our time on earth. Quotations to this effect include:

"The meaning of life is to adventurously discover our gift. The purpose of life is to joyfully share our gift with the world." *Robert John Cook*

"Life is without meaning. You bring meaning to it. The meaning of life is whatever you ascribe it to be. Being alive is the meaning." *Joseph Campbell*

"Whatever we are, whatever we make of ourselves, is all that we have – and that, in its profound simplicity, is the meaning of life." *Philip Appleman*

"There is only one meaning of life: the act of living itself." *Erich Fromm*

"We get to choose the meaning of our lives. Our lives mean exactly what we say they do – no more, no less. Each of us chooses their path in life." *Jonathan Lockwood*

"Purpose is what gives life a meaning." *Charles Henry Parkhurst*

* * * * * * * * * * * * * * * * * *

A fifth of the examples referred to love, and serving humanity, for example:

"The sole meaning of life is to serve humanity." *Leo Tolstoy*

"Our prime purpose in this life is to help others. And if you can't help them, at least don't hurt them." *The Dalai Lama*

"Love is our true destiny. We do not find the meaning of life by ourselves alone – we find it with another." *Thomas Merton*

"I think the meaning of life is, I think it's love." *Julie Benz*

"In our life there is a single colour, as on an artist's palette, which provides the meaning of life and art. It is the colour of love." *Marc Chagall*

"Mother Teresa was asked what the meaning of life was, and she said to help other people, and I thought,

'What a strange thing to say' – but maybe it's the right thing to say." *Jesse Eisenberg*

* * * * * * * * * * * * * * * * * * * *

Some other thoughtful examples include Viktor Frankl's statement that what matters is not the meaning of life in general, but the specific meaning at any given moment, and Charisma Carpenter's opinion that the meaning lies in the journey rather than any one thing or outcome. Janine Shepherd suggested that we should not take ourselves too seriously, but to enjoy the moment, whilst Albert Camus wrote that we shall never be happy if we continue to search for what happiness consists of, and never live if we are looking for the meaning of life.

In summary, these non-religious philosophical statements suggest that there is no ultimate meaning 'out there', so there is no point in wasting time searching for it. Instead, the message is to create your own meaning from your journey through life, and especially through love and service to others.

Humanism is not a religious faith (although, paradoxically, there is a variation known as 'Religious Humanism'), but it is a belief system. Adherents follow a doctrine that denies that we are creations of a deity, but that we should look to science and evolution for answers to questions concerning our existence. There is nothing beyond our own death. They maintain an ethical stance concerned with all that is best about human beings, including civility, generosity, creativity, and empathy. A key tenet is that we have individual freedom, and must each take responsibility for our own lives and for the community.

Secular Humanists declare that the purpose in life is to pursue happiness, grasp the present, live for the moment, and follow the natural way of things. However, they hold that we are all part of a larger existence, should it be family, community, nation, or human species. Because of this, our individual lives have a more enduring meaning, and provide a continuity beyond our own existence.

Whereas Humanists do not generally have anti-religion sentiments, but just maintain that God is not necessary in order to be a moral person, atheists believe that religion is something invented by people to frighten their fellows into following an ethical way of life. Although the boundaries between the two systems are often blurred, according to writer Emma Goldman:

"The philosophy of Atheism represents a concept of life without any metaphysical 'beyond' or 'divine regulator.'"

What do atheists have to offer to help us in our quest to reveal the meaning of life? A trawl through various writings on the subject indicates that they resent any attempt to force on them the notion that a lack of belief in God inevitably leads to degeneration, decay, and a life of pointless pursuits. In response, they state that a caring atheist can find a tremendous meaning and purpose in life. But just what is it?

The answer is that, in contrast to those belief systems that prescribe a purpose, the atheistic position leaves the specifics up to the individual. Logical, scientific theories and facts are there to guide us, rather than unprovable religious superstitions and dogma. The realisation that we are mortal and godless makes each one of our lives invaluable. We are here because, throughout our evolution, the urge to reproduce and propagate the species has been dominant. Our role should be to contribute to making the world a better place during our passage through it.

It would no doubt be difficult for believers and non-believers alike to disagree with many of the above statements on the need to live a morally good life. There can be little more noble than trying and make the world a better place, and to contribute toward society in ways that our individual talents permit. Is there any scope for those with a religious faith add to this? Indeed yes, with the answer dependent on which religion we investigate.

Hinduism may be the world's oldest religion that embraces a personified deity, rather than an earlier worship of objects of nature. It is always difficult to be sure when ancient beliefs and practices began, because they were usually passed on through oral traditions and only written down many years later. The Hindu holy book *Bhagavad-Gita* could have been dictated as long ago as the third millennium before the Christian Era, although it may be more recent. This religion acknowledges many gods, although it can be regarded as form of monotheism through the assimilation of many local divinities into the supreme deity of Vishnu.

Unlike some other views on the meaning of life, Hinduism is quite specific. The goal is to realise the fundamental truth about oneself, through progression of the 'ātman' (soul) across numerous lifetimes until it is liberated from 'kārma' (causal action). The purpose of life is to achieve this by following four guiding principles: to live morally and ethically; to pursue wealth and prosperity within these boundaries; to enjoy one's existence; to achieve enlightenment. The last one is the most difficult, and it may take several lifetimes to accomplish.

Buddhism is a way of life, and not a religion in the specific sense as it does not acknowledge a deity. It was founded in the sixth century before Christ was born, with the belief that all the world's pain was the result of people craving for things that do not bring lasting happiness. Buddhists believe that the purpose of life is to end suffering. This is achieved by embracing 'Four Noble Truths' relating to unproductive pursuits, including that they can be eliminated by following the 'Eightfold Path'. These relate to having the right view, intention, speech, action, livelihood, effort, mindfulness, and concentration. Thus, as with Hinduism, the purpose of life is clearly articulated, but without the involvement of a god.

Judaism dates back to about two millennia before the Christian Era, but again the earliest writings – the first five books, or Pentateuch, of the Hebrew Scriptures (Old Testament) – traditionally held to have been written by Moses, date from at least five hundred years later. The declared meaning of life is to comply with the requirements of the Torah, or laws, believed to have been dictated by God, as contained mainly in these five books. There are 613 of them, and they can be grouped into 248 positives (the do's), and 365 negatives (the don'ts). They include the Ten Commandments, two of which – the prohibition of murder and stealing – are universally enshrined in criminal law.

It may be difficult for pious Jews today to comply with every single law, as some relate to ancient practices such as sacrifice, treatment of slaves, and capital punishment for a surprising number of transgressions. Nevertheless, there are sufficient of them to guide a follower in achieving a righteous and spiritual life on earth.

Islam is the youngest of the great world religions, being founded by the prophet Muhammad who was born in Mecca in or around the year five hundred and seventy of the Christian Era. As is the case with the other religions and belief systems already discussed, Muslims have a specific purpose in life – to obey the 'Five Pillars of Faith'. These concern prayer, fasting, almsgiving, pilgrimage, and profession of faith.

Their holy book, The Quran, contains a great deal of ethical and legal teaching, as well as regulations governing social life such as marriage, divorce, and inheritance. It also makes specific statements on life: mankind was created to be Allah's trustee on earth, and the purpose for man's creation is to worship the creator. Allah is quoted as adding that he made this life in order to test man, so that every person may be recompensed after death for what he has earned.

This brings us finally to the Christian religion, based on the teachings of Jesus in the first century of his Era, as well as the Old Testament. Are adherents of this faith also informed on the meaning of life, or their purpose for being here? The formal answer often given is to seek salvation through the grace of God and intersession of Christ. We must strive to have a relationship with God through his son Jesus, and to bring him glory through adoration, worship, prayer, and study of the Bible. Whilst this seems less specific than are the edicts issued by the other religions, there are also biblical references to guide the follower.

The prophet Micah states that the Lord requires of us to "Act justly and to love mercy and to walk humbly with your God" (6:8). As with the other Abrahamic religions, Christians are urged to keep the Ten Commandments, with emphasis on the first two. When Jesus was asked what one must do to inherit eternal life, he in turn asked the questioner what was written in the law. The man replied by citing the first two Commandments: "Love the Lord your God with all your heart . . . and love your neighbour as yourself" (Luke 10:27). This was the correct answer to the original question.

The Gospel of John gives some hints about our purpose. Those who believe have the right to become children of God (1:12), and they will have eternal life (5:24). Finally, Paul urges us to: "Whatever you do, work at it with all your heart, as working for the Lord, not for human masters, since you know that you will receive an inheritance from the Lord as a reward." (Colossians, 3:23-4).

There can be little disagreement with the exhortations to follow the Commandments, be kind and just to everyone, and to try and live virtuously. However, whilst being rewarded with eternal life is an obvious incentive, the meaning and purpose of life that emerges does seem to be more general than is the case with the other faiths.

Having looked at ideas from all persuasions, is it possible to now draw some conclusions regarding the meaning of life? The answers, if any, will be influenced by how the question is phrased. For example, why were human beings created? Is there a purpose to our existence? Now that we *are* here, what is our role or goal? The next important factor is: is there a creator God? If there is not, then there will be no pre-ordained purpose to our lives.

Our existence may be the result of natural evolution. Atoms combined to form organic molecules in the primordial soup; the molecules randomly clumped together until they, by chance, formed primitive creatures that were capable of replicating themselves – they were alive. Time passed, these creatures gradually became more advanced, adapted to the changing environment, and eventually developed into *Homo sapiens*. Like all animals, there was an urge to survive and to preserve the species rather than deliberately self-destruct.

If this is *how* we were created, then there will be no answer to the question *why*?

Instead, our goal will be driven by the biological urge to reproduce and, despite the war-mongers, to try and avoid destroying the world. Being kind and considerate to others both helps us to achieve this, and also gives us pleasure. The skills and intelligence we have developed have given us a thirst for knowledge and the urge to create new things and explore new places. Eventually we shall each die and be no more, yet will live on through our descendents and the contributions we have made whilst on this earth. Is this the secular answer to the biggest question we can ask?

For those with a religious faith, the answers will be much more specific. We are on

this earth due to the actions of a creator God. Whilst some believe that we were created in our present form, the majority will accept that the mechanisms of natural selection and evolution were used in the process. The non-Christian religions do seem to have quite well-defined goals to achieve in this life, whilst the Christians emphasise glorifying God, seeking salvation, and hoping for the reward of eternal life.

Perhaps we have not found a fully satisfying answer to the 'big question' after all, at least not one that will be universally acceptable. We may each have to just live the best life we can, try to leave the world a better place than it was when we entered it, and bring our own meaning rather than looking for one 'out there'. Those with a religious faith will have more specific guidelines to follow, along with a belief that the secret may be revealed to them in a life hereafter.

Chapter 8

Ageing disgracefully

Why should we try to age gracefully? Surely it is more fun to age **dis**-gracefully! Many years ago the BBC screened a television documentary entitled *Growing Old Disgracefully*. This featured a small group of ladies in their seventies and eighties who were determined not to grow old with the grace normally expected of those in their mature years; they continued to ignore all stereotypes and have as much fun as possible. Although, as will be discussed shortly, the term 'old' is inappropriate, the sentiments expressed in this delightful and heart-warming programme were inspirational in leading me to embark on my own study on this stage of life.

No doubt, like me, you will have opened your newspaper and seen a report of some fantastic research that has 'proved' that eating this or that food is healthy, or that adopting a particular lifestyle can help you to live to be a hundred. The problem is that, whilst some of these findings are genuinely useful, being the outcome of carefully conducted studies, unfortunately others are not. A recent example that has received much publicity – and has caused people to lose confidence in what the 'experts' say – concerns drinking alcohol. Some reports have stated that imbibing any liquor is bad for you, whilst others have extolled the benefits of a glass of red wine a day. Is it surprising that such conflicting statements leave us confused regarding what is the truth?

Before going any further, it is worth noting that the respective influences of genetic factors that we inherit, and therefore cannot do much about now, and the life style we follow that we *can* do something about, is about fifty-fifty. Thus, even if we faithfully obey all the advice we hear on maintaining good health, if it is not in our particular genes that we will live a long and healthy life, then there is little we can do about it – until medical science comes up with a solution.

In order to help us evaluate the worth of the reports we read in the press, a brief outline of the way research is conducted may be helpful. Paradoxically, one problem is that there is just too much of it. Every undergraduate university student has to carry out an original study and produce a dissertation, whilst postgraduates usually spend most of their time on doing research. In addition, practicing academics such as university lecturers are under continuous pressure to continue with such investigations and publish their findings. Indeed, funding for higher education institutions is partly based on its research output.

An important factor in determining how useful the results of a research study may be lies in the way the data were collected and processed. With the 'hard' sciences, such as chemistry, physics and biology, this will usually be by way of an experiment. New chemical or physical processes may be discovered, or a new gene identified that is responsible for a particular medical condition. If these findings can be confirmed by an independent researcher, then they can usually be regarded as reliable.

In the case of the 'softer' social sciences such as psychology or sociology, with which we are mostly concerned here, investigations are often conducted by questionnaires or surveys. Done properly, and with due integrity, meaningful results can often be produced. What can happen, however, is that the pressure on students and academics to carry out and publish studies may lead to short cuts being taken.

Errors can firstly occur because the participant sample was biased, or too small, and did not represent the general population. Then the questions used in the survey may not be reliable or valid; the wording may be ambiguous, and the options for the responses may be confusing and lead to inaccurate scoring. Once all the results have been converted to numbers, they have to be statistically analysed, usually with the aid of a sophisticated computer programme. With this type of survey research, the outcome is almost never a case of 'proving' something beyond any doubt. Instead, the statistics provide an estimate of the probability that the result could have occurred purely by chance. This figure must not be greater than five percent, and preferably only one percent or less.

Unfortunately, the desire to complete the study has been known to tempt researchers to claim significant results when, in reality, there were many opportunities for errors. Many research studies have been conducted with due integrity, and their findings are valid. But, if you have a large enough sample, and accept that the result had as much as a ten percent probability of being achieved by chance, then you can claim to have 'proved' almost anything. Editors of academic journals do not help the situation, as they are generally not interested in accepting research papers that fail to discover anything new, no matter how carefully the study was carried out.

Hopefully, this preamble on how behavioural research should and should not be conducted has made its point. When we read in the press of some new and dramatic discovery has been made – and that includes on how to live a long and happy life – we need to question the way the investigation was carried out, and whether or not the claims stand up to serious scrutiny. If they do, then explaining the mechanism that was responsible for the result is especially important. For example, it might be that low scores on an intelligence test were likely to have been due to poor nutrition, pollution, or drug abuse.

It is now time to look at what we can do to make our time on this earth as enjoyable as possible, and even maybe to extend it. As mentioned earlier, we cannot yet control the genetic influences on our lives, although medical science is starting to do exciting things with genes. What but we can do something about is the fifty percent of factors that are within our own control – our lifestyle and behaviour.

Most of what follows will be based on what psychology has suggested, for that is my own discipline. However, there is some obvious medical advice that we should all follow, such as taking daily exercise, avoiding being overweight, eating a balanced diet, having a good night's sleep, and limiting alcohol intake. It is also advisable to completely avoid all addictive substances, and that includes smoking. Indeed, the first reliable research finding on this was published back in nineteen sixty-two, when a Royal College of Surgeons study found a definite link between smoking and cancer, heart disease, and gastrointestinal problems. Further evidence on the dangers of smoking soon followed, and this convinced me to quit this habit for ever.

Despite all the evidence that medical science has produced, there are still people will who say, for example, that their grandmother smoked like a chimney, or drank like a fish, and still lived to be ninety-seven. Indeed, it is easy to find exceptions to the general rule, but that is what they are – exceptions. Instead, we should look at the majority and, in the case of smoking, the majority who smoke are significantly more likely, than those who don't, to develop a medical problem and die before their time.

So, what do psychologists say that can help us on our merry journey through life, especially in our retirement years? Several years ago, I was driving along a motorway and listening to the radio. A doctor was giving one of his regular talks, dispensing useful pieces of advice. He said something that almost made me immediately stop so that his words could be written down before they disappeared from memory. Luckily, the temptation was resisted, no doubt thereby avoiding a serious traffic accident, but I did make a note as soon as it was safe to do so. He said, "It is a pity we know our own age, otherwise we could just say we were as old as we feel."

Why are we so obsessed with age so that every time somebody is quoted in the media, their age is included? What does it matter if Mrs Jones is fifty-four, or Mr Smith is sixty-one? Are we expected to behave in a certain way just because we reach a particular age? There is no such age as 'old', it is all relative. We can be 'older' or 'younger' than someone else, but there is no ultimate 'old'.

The oldest person to date for which there reliable records was Frenchwoman Jeanne Calment, who died in nineteen ninety-seven aged just over one hundred and twenty-two years. Apart from some biblical figures like Noah, who are said to have lived many hundreds of years, everybody else is young when compared with Madam Calment. Interestingly, the Bible states that our lifetime is limited to one hundred and twenty years (Genesis 6:3), and this agrees closely with current predictions by medical scientists.

Thus, the first lesson in ageing disgracefully is: don't worry about acting your age, or conforming to age-related stereotypes, do whatever you want that is within your capabilities. Cock a snook at conventions, and ignore anyone who says, "Oh, you should not do that at your age." The late George Burns, comedian and actor, who himself became a centenarian, said: "You can't help growing older, but you don't have to get old."

In any event, chronological age is perhaps the least reliable way of assessing how 'old' a person is. In nineteen ninety-seven Dorothy Rogers identified what she called 'frames of reference' to put the meaning of age in perspective. In addition to age in years, these were: psychological age (our feelings, perceptions, attitudes); social age (our roles, habits, activities); physical age (our body posture, appearance, sight and hearing); and developmental age (our view of past, present, and future). Try a little experiment. Let's say your age in years is 65; you regard yourself as being more like those around you who are 60. You enjoy activities with others who are aged about 55. Your physical fitness is more like that of a 60-year old. Using criteria such as when you completed your education, started work, or had children, you regard your stage of life-development as being close to those who are about 58.

Now take the average of these five figures. It comes to 59.6 years. That figure is a more realistic estimate of how old you are than just using how many years you have been on earth. A pity you cannot put this age down on official forms that you have to complete, but then of course you would miss out on your pension and bus pass!

It is time now to debunk all the ridiculous myths and stereotypes that prophets of doom love to attribute to later life, and instead look at all the lovely gains we can enjoy as we grow older. We have already just dealt with the first myth, and concluded that chronological age alone is inaccurate in branding a person as 'old'. The second is that older people are unproductive. There are so many exceptions that it hardly justifies even a passing mention. Political figures have a habit of remaining in office until very late in the accepted lifespan. British Prime Minister Gladstone only retired at eighty-four, and Churchill resigned when he was eighty-one. Hastings Banda of Malawi stood for office at the age of ninety-four. And these are not the only ones.

Among musicians, Verdi composed Othello when he was eighty, and Rubenstein was still playing piano in his nineties. In the sports arena, Ruth Frith won the shot put at the World Masters' games, aged one hundred; John Whittenmore threw the discuss and javelin in a competition when he was a hundred and four, and Baba Joginder Singh was still competing in the discuss event at the age of a hundred and six.

Whilst we cannot all aspire to be athletes, we can all learn new things. Douglas McKeon gained a degree in French when he was eighty-six, Bernard Herzberg started his second masters' degree at the age ninety-six and, at the amazing age of one hundred and seven, Fred Moore was an art student at New Milton, Hampshire. It used to be thought that the human brain ceased to be able to absorb new facts when we are at a certain age, but this is completely untrue. It has been proved beyond doubt that cerebral neurons can develop to store and process new material, no matter how old we are. It may take a bit longer to start learning a new topic, or play an instrument, but it *will* happen. Thus, the old saying: "You are never too old to learn" is perfectly true.

Just think what opportunities this opens up. Instead of just wishing that you knew more about a subject that interests you, or being filled with regret by what you perceive as a missed opportunity to study earlier in life, we can all search for courses that we can take at home, at our own pace, or enquire what is available at local colleges. Learning new things or starting new hobbies is exciting, pleasurable, and rewarding. If you are doing this with others in a class, it is also very sociable and can generate new friendships. Be patient if you seem very slow at first; once the new neurons have time to develop in your brain, the learning process will gradually start to speed up.

Other erroneous notions about later life include the belief that older people become less flexible as they age. This is not true; those who appear to be inflexible will probably have been so throughout their lives. Likewise, we do not become more senile with every passing year; medical records show that only about five percent of those aged sixty-five and older are diagnosed as senile to a greater or lesser extent. Don't let being a bit forgetful make you think that dementia is coming your way.

Just two more myths may be mentioned. One is that the retirement years are all peace, tranquillity, and rocking chairs. In reality, this time of life is often fraught with concerns such as reduced income, declining mobility, loss of friends and family, and having to endure the negative consequences of ageism that pervade society. This can lead to stress, depression, and anxiety that cause older people to withdraw from social contact because they feel powerless, and cannot see a way out.

The final myth is the perception of lack of sexuality. The need for intimacy remains throughout the lifespan, with no abrupt change. There was a charming story and picture in a newspaper some time back about Dudley Read of Sydney, aged eighty-four, marrying Minnie Munro of Scotland, who was one hundred and two. Also in Australia, Les Colley from Melbourne became a father again at the age of ninety-two, but his achievement was recently surpassed by Ramjit Raghav from northern India, who had a child when he was ninety-four – and planned to have more!

We can conclude this discussion with a mention of the gains in later life. Before reading any further, why not jot down all positives of growing older that you can think of; if you are still many years away from this stage, then ask some older friends what they think are the plusses. Here are ten gains that have been identified during surveys:

a) Grandparenting, the opportunity to give and receive unconditional love, and to help guide the new generation.

b) More time can be spent with one's partner and family members.

c) Liberation from the stress of work activities, competition and activities not enjoyed.

d) Opportunities to spend more time on existing interests, and develop new ones.

e) Freedom to pursue education and learning for its own sake.

f) Being able to look back over a long life, have a total perspective of it, and see it as a whole. A good time to write one's memoires.

g) One can now experience the reality of ageing, and accept it, rather than it being an unknown to be feared.

h) Greater spiritual awareness may be experienced, along with an insight into one's place in the universe. The inevitability of eventual death can be accepted with out fear.

i) Opportunities to make significant contributions to the social system concerned with later life. You have personal experience of it, so you can become involved in committees and action groups to bring about change for the better.

j) One type of intelligence – crystallised intelligence – actually improves with age, and so does wisdom.

Did you include any or all of these in your own list? Indeed, the later stage of life is so enjoyable and has so many opportunities to have fun and make contributions that, during a television interview, a young adult said that she could not wait to reach this time herself.

So, in conclusion, if or when you reach what some like to call the 'Third Age' of life, don't think you have to follow any rules or conventions in order to age gracefully, make this the best time of all and, **grow old disgracefully!**

(Note: Some passages in this chapter were previously published in my book 'Growing Old Disgracefully')

Chapter 9

Characters I have met

As we look back over our merry journey through life, the memories of certain people we have met or known invariably keep reoccurring. Inevitably, these will include friends and family who have now sadly departed. In addition to these, there will often be others who have not been close, but nevertheless are memorable for a variety of reasons. No doubt, like me, you may sometimes find yourself saying things like, "Do you remember old so-an-so", or, "I once knew a man/woman who said/did this."

The characters that remain in my mind usually fall into one of three categories, namely: bosses, taxi drivers, and musicians. Those in the first group will form the topic of the later article: 'Bosses I have worked for'. This will include an ex rugby- playing Afrikaner in South Africa. Aside from being a leader who had a heart of gold, he could also put the fear of the Almighty into anyone who crossed him. He also had an amusing way of corrupting certain English expressions. These included his own versions of 'Get your finger out', and the condemnatory value judgement that commences with 'bull'. Certainly an interesting character to work for; he suited me but not everyone who reported to him.

I have been lucky enough to have visited several foreign countries on business, in addition to having had overseas holidays, as well as living abroad for a time. On many occasions, one of the first of the locals that one encounters is a taxi driver, perhaps to get from a cruise terminal or airport to an hotel or business venue. At other times it may be to take a sight-seeing trip around the local sights when only a limited stay is possible. Whilst on holiday, my wife and I have encountered some very nice and helpful drivers who spared no effort to ensure that we saw as many of the local attractions as possible, and at a reasonable cost. Such personalised excursions have often been more successful than organised coach tours – and cheaper.

A business trip to Israel many years ago was particularly memorable for two taxi drivers. The first example occurred after the aircraft landed at Tel Aviv airport late at night, and there did not seem to be a transfer bus to transport passengers to the city centre.

There were a few taxis waiting at the terminal, so I asked one driver to take me to my hotel. He agreed, but asked me to wait to see if he could find another passenger to help fill up his cab – and no doubt increase his income. After what seemed like a long time, he returned empty handed, and we set off.

Seemingly oblivious of any speed limit, he not only drove at a break-neck pace, but spent most of the journey with just one hand on the steering wheel, whilst turning round to talk to me, seated in the back. Tired out at what was probably midnight by that time, all I wanted was to reach the hotel – in one piece – and get some rest before a busy work schedule the next day. "Is this your first visit to Israel?" he asked. Other basic tourist questions followed, and I did my best to answer whilst keeping a nervous eye on the road ahead.

"In this country, all men have to serve time in the armed forces," he said. After I had mumbled something in reply, he continued, "This means that here there are five women to every one man." Again I made some non-committal response. He then said with a twinkle in his eye, "You come to help us out, yes?"

Nice to encounter a cheeky sense of humour, but it would have been appreciated more had it not been long after my bedtime. On one of the few occasions when the driver was looking where he was going, he spotted someone walking by the side of the road, and stopped the car next to them. It was a women soldier, which did rather alter the image of conscription he had painted earlier. He opened the door to let her climb in to the front passenger seat, and then explained to me that there was a custom in Israel for taxis to pick up any uniformed service personnel they see walking, and give them a free ride.

At least this meant he now had somebody else to chat with, and could spend more time looking forward instead of backward. After depositing me at my hotel, he drove off with the woman soldier still on board. Their destination was not revealed to me, but I was in no state to be concerned – a comfortable bed beckoned.

The memory of another taxi driver on this same overseas trip still remains with me. It was a few days later, when I had managed to arrange a Friday free of engagements in order to pay a quick sight-seeing visit to Jerusalem. The outward journey was by a people carrier that held about sixteen passengers, operated by a Jewish transport company. After visiting as many of the famous landmarks as possible within the one day, it was late, and time to think about returning to Tel Aviv. What I had not anticipated was that all Jewish transport ceased when the religious devotions of Shabbat started – which was just before sunset on a Friday, which was now. How was I going to get back to my hotel?

A feeling of genuine concern started to envelop me. After making enquiries from whomever looked like they might be able to help, the advice was to find a taxi operated by an Arab driver, who might be willing to make the journey to Tel Aviv. It became apparent that I was not the only tourist in this predicament, and somehow two or three of us met up in a location where taxis were to be expected. Fortunately, we did find one, and we agreed to share the rather high cost of the trip.

During this journey the driver, like the first one who had driven me from the airport, seemed keen to chat, whether the passengers welcomed this or not. It was a fascinating piece of medical advice that remains in my mind to this day. He said, "I have a miracle treatment for high cholesterol and the heart disease that results from this." We tried to show interest, sceptical of the reference to 'miracle'. Continuing, he said, "You add just five drops of kerosene to a cup of black coffee, and drink it. Do this every day, and you will never encounter a cardiac problem; it will also cure you if you already have one.

Somewhat unconvinced, one passenger asked him how drinking this dubious potion could have such a profound effect. The driver replied with great confidence, "If you have some oil or fat in a container and want to clean it out, then kerosene dissolves it all away. So, if you have fat in your arteries or around the heart, then drinking a little of this liquid will dissolve this also." In order to support his claims, the driver told us of a friend who used to suffer from high cholesterol and the complications that accompanied it. He took this medicine, and is now cured!

We made polite comments to the effect that we would remember this, should it be needed, and the driver was very proud that he had shared such vital, life-saving information with us. If he had been expecting a larger tip from doing so, he was to be disappointed. I strongly doubt that any of my fellow passengers ever availed themselves of this remedy, so please don't try this at home, at least not before first discussing it with your family doctor.

Next, two New York taxi drivers come to mind. One featured when I was on my first business visit to

Chicago in the United States. New York airport was a necessary transit stop to change aircraft, and all I was likely to see of the city was the inside of the terminal building. On the return leg of the journey there was a three-hour wait before my homeward plane departed, so I asked one of the airline staff if there would be time to make a round-trip drive to at least see the famous city skyline. The official was very helpful, and hailed a cab that had just dropped off its fare. He told the driver that I was in transit, with only a limited time available, but was keen to something of the sights. After all, you can hardly boast that you have been to an overseas location if all you had seen was the airport.

One would think that the driver would have been pleased to have such a customer, but he hesitated. He said that it cost twenty bucks an hour to hire the cab, but he would not receive as many tips in one long journey as he would in several shorter ones within the same period. What a mercenary response! However, I said that I had some travellers' cheques left that would more than cover any potential loss to him. He replied that these would have to go to his employer, as they were no use to him as a gratuity. After searching through my wallet, I told him that I still had some dollars left, and he could have these as a tip. On hearing this, he finally agreed to take me on the little tour.

Although it was not the most auspicious of starts, the driver warmed to his task, and gave a commentary on which borough we were going through, and pointed out any landmarks of interest. Unfortunately, the weather was not very good and there was some drizzle and mist in the air. The only glimpse of the skyline we had was when we were on an elevated highway running past the city, but my camera was at the ready, and a photograph confirmed that I had indeed visited the Big Apple.

The driver even pulled off the road onto a track near an impressive bridge. Was I going to be robbed and then abandoned, out of sight of passing motorists? But no, he just wanted to show me the view. The bridge was the Brooklyn and, looking seawards, there in the distance was the Statue of Liberty. I took a photograph of him standing next to the bridge, with the statue just visible behind him, and he took one of me. After this, we made our way back to the airport, and I gave the driver the travellers' cheques and all the local currency I had left. He said he was satisfied, so everyone was happy.

The other New York example was when my wife and I made a brief visit to the city, after flying there from Iceland. We were to travel back to the UK on the *Queen Victoria* cruise liner, and a taxi had been arranged to take us to the ocean terminal. Although not a long distance, driving across the grid system of busy roads was a slow, stop-start journey. The driver was keen to make conversation, whether we wanted to or not, and started off with a comment about a visit the Pope was currently making somewhere. He later admitted that he was testing us to see whether or not we were as interested in the topic of religion as he was.

At least it passed the time away as we waited at one traffic light after another. Our courier had quite strong ideas on the state of the world, and how many of the global problems could be solved if people followed the biblical teachings. He was right, of course, but this would be no easy task when different religions were squabbling and fighting among themselves. Maybe he was an evangelist, and was taking advantage of the chance to talk to the many people he would meet during his working day. Good luck to him, if this was the case and he wished to spread the message of peace and goodwill.

For a long time, and especially on having heard inspired religious singing by the local choirs in Africa, I have had a wish to experience gospel singing in a Harlem church. Our driver was an African-American, and I asked him, probably naively, if a Caucasian like me would be permitted to enter one of these buildings. He replied that I would be welcomed, but that I should be aware that it would probably be a Pentecostal service. Thus, it would be charismatic and there would be speaking in tongues. Perhaps he thought that this might be a bit 'over the top' for someone he might have perceived of as a rather staid Englishman. However, there would be no opportunity to explore this now, as the taxi had just driven past the prow of the *Queen Victoria*, and was about to deposit us at the drop-off zone at the cruise terminal.

The final group of memorable characters for me is made up of jazz musicians. There must be something about this art form that brings out the zaniness in those who practice it. The first example I can recall was a double bass player, 'KM'. He was much older than me, a good player, and something of an intellectual. "Never be without a book in your pocket," he used to say, "And never waste the chance to read it when you are on a bus, or waiting for someone." He tended to do odd things, usually unexpectedly.

Once he was talking to two of us by a main road; it was growing dark, and cars were driving by with their lights on. He then saw one that was still unlit, and immediately pulled out his cigarette lighter, stuck out his arm as the vehicle was passing, and waved the flame at the motorist. We thought this was highly amusing, even though it was done in the interest of road safety. I cannot recall if the driver took the hint or even understood the gesture – other than to think he was being confronted by a nut case.

Then there was – and still is at the time of writing – a versatile musician, 'BD', who played the drums in a small group to which I also belonged. A life-long bachelor, he developed a rather eccentric personality all of his own. When he went in his car to visit people, he usually timed it to arrive at meal times. Of course the decent thing to do, especially knowing that he had no wife waiting at home for him, was to invite him to join the family for a meal. Obviously prepared for this, he always carried a tin of ham in his vehicle, and promptly offered to fetch it so he could contribute to the fare. I don't think anyone ever accepted this 'goodwill gesture', so the tin must have survived to a great age before it was consumed – if it ever was.

Whenever he was telephoned at home, 'BD' was invariably preparing some food for himself whilst carrying on the conversation. On one occasion he was making something on toast, and the clattering of pots and pans could be heard in the background. The food often suffered during this multi-tasking effort and, after an obvious sound of muttering and scraping, my friend announced with a sigh, "You may like to know the score: it is toast one, BD nil!" Only recently I telephoned to wish him a Happy Christmas. Again he was in the kitchen attempting to make some food. It was only a short conversation, but the background culinary noises were there again. After a minute or two he announced, "Oh, now I have gone and burnt the soup!" Some things never change, do they.

Finally, there was 'SK' the funniest man I have ever had the privilege to know, sadly no longer with us, but no doubt entertaining the angels up above. He was an inaugural member of a little jazz band a few of us formed near the start of this millennium. His role was playing the banjo, but he was also a pianist. During his time with us he created some musical arrangements in the style of the old Dixieland tunes.

Although he did not tell jokes as such, he had a way of relating anecdotes that was hilarious. Given a chance to strum his instrument and sing quietly along with it, even his rendition of well-known little folk ditties had us all in fits of uncontrollable laughter. If ever one needed proof of the old adage concerning humour that 'it is not what you say but the way that you say it', then you only had to listen to this delightful man.

Of course, he may have used a bit of poetic licence with his anecdotes, so perhaps one should not take them too literally. One of his most hilarious stories concerned his early days as a member of the entertainment staff of a well-known holiday camp. These people had to be versatile, and be able to turn their hands to many tasks including organising sports, quizzes and games, and whatever else was required to keep the campers happy.

One day, his boss asked him if he could play a musical instrument. If he could not, then his job with the camp would have to come to an end. Although at that time he was not a musician, he answered that, yes, he was indeed an instrumentalist. "Then bring it with you tomorrow, and play along with the pianist who accompanies the sing-along sessions," his boss replied.

Wondering what to do about this, but not wishing to be faced with losing his job, that afternoon SK visited all the second-hand shops in the nearby town, and spied a banjo in one of the windows. He bought it, and then purchased a self-tutor book to try and learn how to play it. On that first day, he learnt the chord of 'C-major' which, as musical readers will know, is the most basic and common chord that a beginner has to master. However, songs are written in any one of several keys, not just 'C', and, even when they are, they contain more than just this one chord.

Our friend said that he went to see the pianist, and explained his situation. She was a kindly woman who understood the demands of holiday camp life. SK asked if she could play every song in the key of 'C', so that he could at least strum along with his one chord, hoping that it would fit in for at least some of the time. The pianist agreed, and they played the first sing-along duo, and apparently satisfied the boss that SK was indeed a musician.

As the days went by, he learned more chords, and eventually became very accomplished on the banjo but, without the threat of dismissal all those years earlier, he might not have discovered the joys of being a musician. Dear SK, people like him don't come along very often.

Chapter 10

Peak emotional experiences

Have you ever had an experience, not induced by any substance or medication you may have taken, where you seemed to be elevated to an altered state, or higher plane of consciousness? These episodes are usually accompanied by feelings of profound joy, revelation, insight, or of being at one with the world. If you can relate to this, then you are not alone. Examples relating to such unusual or mystical events have been reported in the writings of both Eastern and Western religions from the earliest of times. One manifestation, that of inner voices, was described by the ancient Egyptians, Greeks and Romans, including the philosopher Socrates (c.470-399 BCE) who heard them throughout his life.

Interest among serious researchers was stimulated in the nineteen-sixties by American psychologist Abraham Maslow. He regarded the ability to achieve 'peak' experiences' as one of the characteristics of human beings who had successfully fulfilled the highest level of innate needs, which he called 'self-actualisation'.

Not only could they be triggered by true spiritual enlightenment, they could also originate from great moments of love and sex, natural childbirth, bursts of creativeness, moments of discovery, fusion with nature, and athletic accomplishments.

Of particular interest are aesthetic events, particularly music, that were also highlighted by Maslow. Although peak experiences usually come unexpectedly, he commented that some individuals could rely on certain tunes to help bring them about. We all have access to music, so it is a good medium to use for research, as will be discussed shortly.

Just to clarify what is being discussed here, you may have come across different terms that can mean the same thing as Maslow described. These include occurrences that are variously described as transpersonal, mystical, anomalous, optimal, numinous, or 'flow'. It is often difficult to differentiate the specific meanings of these so, for the purposes of this article, they will all be subsumed under the heading 'Peak Emotional Experiences', from hereon abbreviated to PEEs.

Perhaps surprisingly, surveys have shown that PEEs are not particularly rare. In the nineteen-seventies,

Alister Hardy in the United Kingdom widely publicised a request for information. He invited people to respond if they had been aware of, or influenced by, a presence or power, whether they called it God or not, which was different from their everyday self. If they had, then what were they doing at the time? His analysis of the first three thousand questionnaires showed that twenty-one different activities or mental states had been listed that had preceded the experience. Depression or despair were the ones most often mentioned, with prayer or meditation second, and perception of natural beauty third.

Other studies have likewise yielded high levels of affirmative responses, including sixty-five per cent of a sample of UK students, and forty-eight per cent of those surveyed from the national population. In America, Andrew Greeley asked nearly fifteen hundred adults: "Have you ever felt as though you were very close to a powerful spiritual force that seemed to lift you out of yourself?" Thirty-five per cent said that they had, and nearly half of these cited music as the most frequent trigger.

PEEs go hand-in-hand with being totally absorbed in an activity, to such an extent that the individual becomes oblivious to what is going on around him or her – the rest of the world simply does not exist. It is easy to see how such a state can heighten the senses and give the impression that one has been elevated to a higher level of consciousness than is normally experienced. It is likewise understandable that those who are deeply religious, and have achieved their PEE through meditation or devotional pursuits, will feel closer to their God.

Do you think it is possible to be so passionate about music that playing or listening to it will lead to this total absorption, and the resulting 'peak'? It was the desire to explore this that led me to conduct a series of research studies, using several hundred volunteers from the staff of the UK university at which I was employed as a psychology lecturer.

The first phase paralleled those carried out by others, as mentioned earlier, namely: how common are PEEs? To broaden the scope, my questionnaire firstly asked participants if they had experienced one or more of these when they were performing some physical activity. The question was then repeated to explore this in a passive condition, such as sitting, relaxing, listening to music or prose, meditation, or close personal relationships.

Inevitably with such research, not everyone returned the survey but, of the almost three hundred and fifty who did, about three quarters of them admitted to having had such an experience in either one condition or the other, and often in both. The most frequent triggers for the active condition were doing something creative, problem solving (including mathematical), and competitive sport or athletic pursuit. Nearly twelve per cent of the participants stated they were playing a musical instrument at the time.

The main antecedent for the passive condition was listening to music. This was followed by daydreaming or being half awake, and then by close personal relationships. When the triggers for both conditions were combined, music was found to be the one most frequently mentioned overall. Just one final statistic: half those who responded said the experience had changed them in a positive way, whilst most of the remainder reported no change or that it was too early to tell.

How and why do so many people have these experiences, where they seem to lose touch with the present and enter an altogether higher level of consciousness or reality? Perhaps it is impractical to assume that the mechanisms are the same for all the triggers. Those who have had such an encounter whilst being engaged in spiritual meditation or religious events, will probably claim that a supernatural source was responsible.

Whatever the trigger, sacred or secular, the general belief is that during these episodes the external world is either distorted or excluded, and internal thoughts and feelings are brought to the fore with enhanced clarity and insight.

This brings us again to music. Not only was it mentioned by Maslow as a common antecedent, but it was also the one most frequently mentioned by the present participants. What is so special about music that it has the power to induce such profound experiences? Various experts have offered opinion which, when combined, suggest that it is a special form of non-verbal communication that appeals directly to the 'soul', and forms a bridge to the inner, spiritual world. It may even have pre-dated speech, with its origin being in the musical vocalisations that mothers did, and still do, make to their babies to encourage the emotional bonding so important to survival. It became clear that more research into the role of music and peak experiences was indicated.

Over one hundred members of the original sample agreed to complete another questionnaire, this time specifically about their involvement with music. Whilst not everybody admitted to being strongly musical, those who did reported that listening to it often caused physical sensations ('I can feel it in my stomach'), and they felt that they were addicted to it. They also found themselves trying to analyse the composition as it was being played. Those who were less musical often just reported cheerful responses, such as singing or whistling along to the tune. Thus, those for whom music was important experienced deeper and more profound reactions than did the superficial ones of their less musical colleagues.

Seventy-four of the participants who had helped with the research so far were willing to stay with it for the next phase. This was to see if PEEs could be triggered under laboratory conditions. Two, thirty-minute recorded selections of music were prepared, one designated 'gentle' comprising pieces by composers such as Elgar and Mozart, and the second 'upbeat' with numbers by the likes of Wagner and Stravinsky. Only classical instrumental tunes were used, as these are usually more complex in structure than are the more contemporary, popular compositions. They also eliminated the effect of human communication that could occur with vocalised songs.

To avoid possible distractions, a comfortable room containing high quality audio equipment was used for this study. There was also a computer that had been programmed with custom-written software, which was connected to a hand-held button that registered elapsed time whenever it was pressed. The participants firstly heard one of the music selections, and pressed the button if and when they had experienced a PEE. Several weeks later, they returned and repeated the exercise with the other set of recorded pieces.

Although there was some apprehension about whether any PEEs would result from an experimental condition like this, over three quarters of those who took part pressed the button at least once when listening to one or other music selection. Usually this was done more frequently, and occasionally even as often as thirty or forty times. The upbeat tunes generated significantly more responses than did the gentle ones.

The question now was, would it be possible to identify what aspects of the music could have caused people to experience these feelings. A colleague who was a lecturer, conductor and composer was asked to help with this endeavour.

We concentrated on the places in the music where the computer records indicated the incidences of button pressing were highest. For the upbeat selection, most peaks occurred at the start of a rousing passage, the impacts of a gong and bass drum (in Copland's *Fanfare for the Common Man*), the beginning of a build up to a crescendo, and a powerful ensemble section. In the case of the more gentle music, the start of a climax sequence, the entry of a different solo instrument, a change to a 'dark' minor section, and the first obvious fortissimo, all resulted in an increase in PEEs. The greatest number of peaks for any selection was the stirring conclusion to Stravinsky's *Firebird Suite*.

The findings indicated two other interesting things. Firstly, it appeared that listeners who experienced multiple peaks needed some time to recover from one before they were able to experience another. It was as if an emotional saturation point was reached, and that this could not be sustained. Thus, it needed to dissipate before susceptibility to more peaks returned. The other observation was that both upbeat *and* gentle music were able to bring about PEEs. It was, therefore, not just a case of these being triggered by arousal, as many researchers had thought. We speculated that the slower, quieter pieces, if of sufficient merit, may have led to a dreamy state of introspection, and stimulated memories of peaceful scenarios. This in turn could result in raising the level of consciousness above that normally experienced in the mundane world around us.

There remained just one more experiment to conduct: what is going on in the brain during a PEE? Artistic pursuits, including music, are processed mainly in the right side of the brain, whereas logic and reasoning are concentrated in the left hemisphere. However, some researchers have opined that, in order to achieve what we are here calling PEEs, both parts of the brain must be involved. It would have been wonderful if funding had been available to use the most up-to-date brain scanners to conduct my own study but, alas, the university's budget could not be stretched to facilitate this. Did this mean that this multi-stage investigation into the power of music would come to an end?

'Nothing ventured, nothing gained', as the old saying goes. A company called Oxford Instruments, UK, Ltd very kindly agreed to help out by bringing an electroencephalograph (EEG) machine to the university for a day, along with two technicians. This only allowed for eight of the long-suffering original participants to be wired up with twenty-one electrodes on their heads, and listen again to a music selection, armed with the hand-held button to press if they experienced a 'peak'.

The results were not available instantly. With a growing sense of excitement, a few days later I drove down to the company's headquarters in Oxford itself, to watch the analysis of the brain scans. Using a sophisticated computer programme, the first step was, for each participant, to insert markers on the tracings of the brain waves where the PEE button had been pressed, if indeed this had occurred. The technician than converted the ten seconds of activity preceding the marker into a brain map. If there were several peaks for a participant, the results were pooled in order to combine as many such segments as possible.

The resulting image was an outline of the top of the head, with the main areas of brain activity shown in different colours depending on their intensity. Gradually, the maps for all the eight participants were created. Would these reveal the outcome we were hoping for?

Well, after all that anticipation, the results from this limited pilot study were mixed. Two participants had recorded few or no peaks that could be used for the analysis, and the tracings from another four did show some arousal but the EEG signals had been 'contaminated' by 'noise' interference. This left just two useful brain maps and, joyfully, they both showed just what we were anticipating: evidence of only right brain involvement with 'normal' listening, but heightened activity in both the left and right hemispheres in the run up to a PEE.

Thus, mission accomplished, if only in a limited way. It would be wonderful to be able to repeat these brain scans with many more people, in order to confirm what must be regarded as tentative findings. Nevertheless, the complete study had shown that these peak emotional experiences are not rare, that they can be triggered by music, even under laboratory conditions, and that they probably involve the whole brain. For those wishing to explore a mental state where we seem to be transported to a higher level of consciousness, music can provide a safe stimulus to launch us on this fascinating voyage.

Chapter 11

Does graphology work?

Graphology can be formally defined as the alleged science of divining personality from handwriting. You will see that the word 'science' has been preceded by 'alleged' because, for it to be accepted as such a discipline, it must be shown to have predictive ability and be based some objective criteria. In other words, it needs to be able to measure psychological traits that are believed to underlie some aspects of behaviour, and then confirm through observation that this behaviour actually occurs. Attempts thus far to validate graphologist's claims have led to mixed results.

The rules for classification of the handwriting characteristics that these practitioners use today were first laid down in the late eighteen-eighties by a Frenchman called Jean Crepieux-Jamin. Since then, text books have been published for both the serious student and the popularist market. The authors of such texts are quite serious about their claims that personality traits, or types of intellectual ability, can be identified. They maintain that many graphology signs exist that prove reliable, based on anecdotal evidence, or have been discovered by experience. However, explanations for their predictive ability are hard to find.

There are many types of handwriting elements that are examined when performing an analysis. They include how and where the 'i' is dotted and the 't' is crossed, the shape of the stem below the line of letters such as 'p' and 'q', and of those above the line like 'b' and 'd'. Taking the sample as a whole, there is the matter of how much hand pressure was used, and whether or not the letters are sloped. If they are, then is the slope forward or backward? Consideration is also given to the quantity and type of flourishes and embellishments in the script.

The inclusion of handwriting analysis in applied contexts such as job selection is already popular in France and Israel, and is increasing in several other countries. But does research confirm that this is justified? In one study, over a hundred personnel were assessed using graphology, along with other criteria such as supervisor ratings, self ratings, and productivity. The conclusion from this was that handwriting analysis was not a viable method of assessment.

Other studies included one where bank employees were rated on several traits, including hand-written biographies, and another where successful employees were judged on the basis of graphometric analysis. The agreements between the script characteristics and the other personnel ratings were found to be very weak, or not significantly better than chance. With regard to the inclusion of graphology in the selection process, several investigators have reviewed data from a range of earlier published studies, and concluded that this form of assessment does not successfully predict future performance in the work-place.

Despite such negative reports, there are others that provide more positive evidence. Taking a somewhat different approach, one study obtained scripts from groups of individuals who were already successful in a variety of occupations, including business, actors, and nuns. The graphologists were challenged to allocate the anonymous authors to their appropriate profession, and were successful on sixty-five per cent of occasions. The same task carried out by a control group of non-graphologists achieved a slightly lower success rate of fifty-nine per cent. In another trial, raters were successful at a level greater than chance, in matching graphological reports with undergraduate students known to them.

A study of particular interest to me, in view of some original research that will be discussed shortly, was reported by Stanley Oosthuizen. It was on graphology as a predictor of academic achievement among second-year university students. The participants were asked to create a short, hand-written assignment, unaware that these would be used later for analysis. They also completed a standardised personality questionnaire that assessed personal relations, home relations, social relations, and formal relations. The students' handwriting was then analysed for the presence of ten components, including the upper and lower zones of the letters, gradient of the lines, and slant.

The researcher then separately used the findings of both tests as predictors for the end-of-year grade points awarded for psychology. When all the results were available, it was found that the personality test results had no predictive value. Although in total the graphology analyses outcomes were likewise not significant, two individual elements did yield positive findings greater than chance. They were the upper zone of the letters, and the waviness of the lines of writing.

The former may not have been unexpected, as the upper zone is held by graphologists as being the area of intellect, ambition, and ideals. For example, a high cross bar of a letter 't' is significant, especially if it is also sloping upwards. However, the lack of straight lines being a predictor is puzzling. A uniform direction of writing is believed to indicate emotional stability, but waviness suggests hesitation, instability, and anxiety. Was this finding just a non-significant anomaly?

In view of the dearth of impartial research on the claims made for graphological analysis, and the often lack of significant support for those that have been carried out, it seemed opportune to conduct an original study to try and obtain a definitive outcome. Several factors made this a feasible project. Firstly, I was working as a university lecturer, with access to students' hand-written assignment scripts, as well as facilities for computer-aided analyses. Secondly, a professional graphologist had agreed to use her skills to assess the samples. As a guiding principle, we based our work on the assumption that specific components of handwriting would be associated with personality characteristics that predispose a person to academic achievement.

There were four aspects to this study. We obtained one hundred first-year undergraduate examination scripts from psychology students who had since left the college. Over half of these were from participants who were aged nineteen or twenty at the time, although in total the range extended up to forty-six years of age. Nearly three quarters of the examinees were female, which reflects the popularity of this subject for women. Each of the papers had originally been graded by the subject tutor and, as was the usual practice, some were second-marked by another member of the department.

For the first of our investigations, we selected one question from the examination paper, and arranged for each of the answers to this be typed out. These copies were then marked by current tutors, so that we could compare the grades awarded for the printed version with those originally allocated to the hand-written scripts. The markers would not be the same as those who performed the original gradings, but we were confident that the marking guides that are always prepared by the question compilers would lead to reliable assessments of the students' responses. The purpose of this was to see if the grades awarded could have been influenced by either the neatness or untidiness of the writing; those in the latter category would have been more difficult to read.

In order to accomplish our second aim, it was necessary to select some handwriting features that were simple, objective, and primary, rather than being subjective or just providing an overall impression that might be difficult to replicate. A computer programme created for this study enabled previously scanned pages of scripts to be displayed within a window on the screen. Measurements could then be made on the images, based on pixel separation. Using vertical and horizontal lines that were included in the programme, we were able to accurately record aspects of letter height (such as 'l' and 'f'), width (from the 'o'), and the average slant of the writing both above and below the line.

Thirdly, we had to agree on what characteristics of the writing that could be assess by the graphologist, were held to be indicators of academic performance. A compromise had to be reached between what skills a pool of psychology tutors considered were necessary, and what could be discretely identified through the handwriting analysis. Eventually, the following twelve characteristics were adopted: concentration, application, a clear mind, conscientiousness, carefulness, ambition, constancy, imagination, ability to see the essential of a problem, receptivity, meticulousness, and logical ability.

Those of us who are not accomplished in the practice of graphology may wonder how these traits are identified. I can only answer by quoting from the manual. 'Concentration', for example, is apparently indicated by writing that is small or mostly condensed, in relief, dots close to the stem, and weak upper and lower extensions. 'Application' is evident by firm, regular, stable baseline, orderly, simple, poised, angular, and resolute. People who are creative form full and original letters, in relief, effervescent, with well-developed loops and ovals, playful movements, and an abundance of curves. We decided to simply score each of these as being 'present' or 'absent' for each of the script samples.

Fourthly and finally, the graphologist was asked to use any of the techniques available to her in order to make an overall judgement on whether the student would have passed or failed. She did not have the full response to the question, only a single page as a sample of the writing. There would, therefore, have been only a small indication of the academic content of the answer to inform the decision, either consciously or subconsciously.

It is time now to consider what we found in answer to the question: can graphology accurately predict academic performance? Firstly, how did the marks for the typewritten versions compare with those for the original handwritten ones? Although there was a significant correlation between the two sets of marks, the agreement was not total. The average grade for the typed version was forty-three percent, whilst that for the handwritten ones was nearly forty-eight percent. This suggests that the original tutors were marking for content, and were not unduly influenced by the neatness or any other quality of the writing. Whilst this is pleasing to know, other factors could have affected this finding, including the fact that different markers were used for the two sets of scripts.

Our second aim was to see if our objective measurements of letter size and slant could be related to the examination grades. The only factor to show a significant, modest, correlation was writing that had a uniform slant, regardless of whether it was forward or backward. Letter height or width appeared to be irrelevant.

The presence or absence of the twelve writing characteristics that were suggested as possibly having a bearing on academic performance, and which could be assed by graphology, were compared with the grade points. We found that writing that was both careful and consistent was significantly related to examination performance. Just twenty-eight percent of the sample fell into this category. Taken individually, both these two factors just failed to be statistically significant, and the other ten items in the list were completely insignificant.

This just leaves us with the global opinion on which students had passed or failed. The graphologist was able to offer an opinion on only forty-five of the hundred scripts, but was remarkably accurate with her predictions on these. She correctly identified thirty-seven students who had been successful. Whilst impressive, the fact that no opinion was forthcoming for fifty-five of the cases does reduce the overall usefulness of obtaining predictions in this way.

What conclusions can be drawn from this multi-stage study to investigate the validity of graphology as a meaningful scientific discipline? Perhaps the most significant finding was that writing that was both careful and constant was associated with higher examination marks. The relevance of carefulness in handwriting is, however, fairly evident and is seen as a relatively neat typographical style, regular, controlled, and with clear spacing and legibility. The same can be said of writing that has a regular rather than a mixed slant, as found in our computer-aided measurements.

Does this indicate a potential source of marking bias from tutors who have to read hundreds of scripts from the same student cohort? Are they likely to award higher grades to the scripts that are easy to read? Whilst it is tempting to make this assumption, the trial with typed versions of the answers did not confirm this; if anything the reverse occurred. However, the use of different tutors in the marking of the two sets of answers may have influenced these results. Even if the same tutors had been available, there would then have been the potential bias of them remembering what marks they had previously awarded.

It is not known what criteria the graphologist used to make the overall pass or fail decisions, but the accuracy of the verdicts on the forty-five scripts attempted was significant. Whilst this is worthy of further investigation, there remains the possibility that the content of even the short extracts of students' answers, and the readability of the handwriting, could have influenced the decisions. This may only have occurred subconsciously, but it cannot be completely ruled out.

Taking all the findings together, perhaps the most that can be tentatively claimed for this type of analysis is that those who write neatly, orderly, controlled, firm, and carefully executed scripts, with a consistent slope if there is one, have the best chance of achieving high marks. Perhaps those who can write like this are also orderly and controlled in other aspects of their lives, including preparation for examinations.

As regards the numerous specific elements of handwriting that graphologists use in their assessments, in order to make judgements on aspects of personality or potential job performance, these have yet to be confirmed by controlled experiments and blind trials. It is thus unfortunate that candidates who attend job interviews may be subjected to such an examination, and that their success or failure in obtaining a position may depend on the outcome of these.

Chapter 12

The happiness formula

If we are to believe what we sometimes read in the press, lurking somewhere out there, but still evading capture, is a formula that will guarantee happiness. Just like the desire to find the secret of a long life (see the earlier article: 'Ageing disgracefully'), happiness is a popular subject for researchers who want to achieve fame and fortune (or at least an academic publication) by discovering how to attain it.

Even the United Kingdom Government decided to join the hunt, conducting over several years what they called the 'Personal Well-being in The UK' survey. The results showed that the average rating for happiness increased from 7.29 out of 10 in the year two thousand and twelve to 7.51 in two thousand and seventeen. The main contributing factors included personal relationships, health, what we do, finance, and education. During the year following, the score rose again slightly. Whether or not the Government is making good use of these findings is not overtly obvious at the time of writing!

It would serve little purpose to review all the findings that have been published on what makes us happy, but just two studies are worth mentioning. They are useful because they are both 'longitudinal', meaning that factors measured earlier in life were then related to what happened to the participants many years later, even including how long they lived. The first of these investigations is known as 'The Harvard Study'. Between the years nineteen thirty-nine and nineteen forty-two, two hundred and sixty-eight male undergraduate students at Harvard University in the USA were recruited. They were aged nineteen or twenty on commencement, and were given tests and questionnaires to complete. All but twenty of them continued to be assessed every five years for the next sixty years, and this included a physical examination.

The researchers were interested to see if certain factors that were present before the age of fifty could predict a long and happy life. Some very interesting results emerged. Firstly, successful agers were those who took control over their smoking, drinking, exercise, body weight, education and marital stability.

They also used what the investigators called 'mature coping mechanisms', indentified as: anticipating potentially stressful events; holding back unacceptable emotions; being altruistic; diverting energy from inappropriate impulses to socially acceptable ones; having the ability to use humour and see the funny side of things.

In contrast, those who reported lower life satisfaction and who had died at a younger age than did the successful group, did not control their life style, and used 'immature coping mechanisms'. These included: using passive aggression and masochism; being a hypochondriac; outwardly acting out their feelings; dissociating themselves from, or denying, problems; projecting their feelings onto other people; using their imagination to create a false self-concept.

No studies of this nature are free from potential error, and other factors could have influenced the findings. Nevertheless, we would do well to try and follow the example of the successful agers if we want to increase our chances of achieving happiness and longevity.

The other piece of research that will benefit from a mention here was on women, and it also covered a sixty-year span. However, unlike the Harvard Study that by necessity was continued by successive generations of academics, rather then the original team, this one was completed by a single researcher. Does this sound improbable? It is called 'The Nun Study', and it was conducted in a quite a novel way. In the year nineteen ninety-one, it was discovered that nuns, when they were originally admitted to the American School Sisters of Notre Dame, had been asked by the then Mother Superior to write their autobiographies. This was during the years nineteen thirty-one to nineteen forty-three, when the women were aged from eighteen to thirty-two.

One hundred and eighty of the nuns were still alive when the research commenced, and they agreed to be periodically tested for cognitive ability that would indicate the presence of Alzheimer's dementia. This continued until the year two thousand, when the surviving participants were then aged from seventy-five to ninety-five. The ages of those who had died were also recorded. The autobiographies were then analysed for factors such as cognitive function, idea generation, and the presence of words that indicated positive, negative, and neutral emotions that the nuns had used when describing their childhood and family experiences.

It was found that those who had scored poorly on cognitive ability as young adults had the highest risks of developing Alzheimer's disease in later life. It was as if education and other mental stimulation early in life provided a 'cognitive reserve' that protected the women from dementia as they grew older. Another key discovery was that those who used positive emotions in their autobiographies tended to live an average of eight years longer than those who did not. This remarkable finding is difficult to explain, but it does suggest a link between mental and physical health, especially with regard to cardiovascular problems. Once again, you will recall this connection being mentioned in the 'Ageing disgracefully' article.

Before bringing together all the factors that have been shown to help us be happy, and compiling a formula, it would be remiss to not mention some research findings relating to religion. It is not the intention here to try and evangelise, or advocate one faith over others, but simply to state in an open-minded way the outcome of some studies.

There is much evidence to show that joining in worship with others can help people cope with life's adversities. In two thousand and three, an investigation by W. DuWayne Battle and Ellen Idler identified several benefits from attending religious services with others, which were not present with private prayer and meditation. These included obtaining a sense of refreshment, cleansing, serenity, beauty, and unity. Others have found a relationship between spiritual experiences and the reduction of medical symptoms. Harold Koenig showed from several studies that, by praying to God and believing that he is capable of intervening, hospital in-patients older than sixty years felt that they are doing something to improve their situation. Remarkably, he also found that participating in religious services might be associated with increased longevity of up to seven years.

It is time now to summarise all the factors that are believed to contribute to personal happiness. These are mostly taken from published studies, including some with which I have been personally involved. Before reading on, however, you may wish to pause for a moment and compile your own list, and then compare it with what follows. Please note that they are not shown in any order of priority.

1) A Good Meal

As we grow older, there are many things that we can no longer do, but we can still look forward to a special meal (especially if it cooked by somebody else!), enjoy it at the time, and then look back on it with happy memories. Unfortunately, this contribution to happiness does not last for ever, and to repeat the experience too frequently will have an adverse effect on the waist-line!

2) A Nice holiday

The happiness resulting from this might last a little longer than that generated by a good meal, as in this case we have had the pleasure of planning and anticipating the holiday, and then savouring the memories and photographs afterwards – unless it rained all the time. However, we are not permanently on holiday, and would probably be complacent about it if we were. Returning to our familiar routine can be pleasurable in itself.

3) Entertainment

The enjoyment we obtain from a special meal or a holiday can also apply to going to a live show, watching a good programme on television, or listening to our favourite music. There is much evidence to confirm that music can trigger a profound feeling of pleasure. If we are a musician, actor, or chorister, then actually performing *with* others, *for* others who enjoy it, can be a truly uplifting experience. The role of music will be discussed further in a later article.

4) Work and Other Activities

Work can be full-time, part-time, voluntary, or involvement with a charity, as well as being a homemaker, parent, grandparent, or carer. If we enjoy doing these things, and feel that what we accomplish is meaningful and satisfying, then this will make us happy. In a series of studies carried out by the Department of Occupational Therapy at The University of Northampton, with which I was involved, we asked retired people what passive and active pursuits they engaged in purely for pleasure.

For men, we found that the main *passive* activities, in order of frequency, were: watching television; listening to the radio; reading. For the women they were the same but in a different order: reading; watching television; listening to the radio. Turning now to the *active* pursuits, for men these were: sport; walking; gardening. The women again responded with the same ones but ranked them differently: gardening; walking; sport. One other pursuit was ranked highly by both men and women, and that was engagement in altruistic activities, particularly voluntary work.

Regardless of the type of activity, it is important that the level of engagement in it is right for you; having either too little to do (bored) or too much (stressed), detracts from happiness rather than enhances it.

5) Health

This is an obvious factor to include, and no doubt you, the reader, will have included this in your own list. If we feel unwell and believe that our health is threatened, then we will be unhappy. Some people complain all the time about their health issues, which in reality may often be minor. Others, who can have quite severe disabilities, nevertheless are always cheerful and try to live life to the full without complaining. We can think of these as 'cup half full' people, compared with the miserable individuals who are 'cup half empty'. Being prepared to carry on regardless, to adapt to changing circumstances, and continue to do things that give pleasure, plus sharing a good laugh whenever possible, is no doubt part of the secret of happiness.

6) Social Relationships

Research has confirmed the importance of good social relationships with family and friends. We are a gregarious species, not a solitary one; we obtain much happiness from interacting with others, and being a part of the greater whole of humanity where we love and are loved. If we are lonely, we are unhappy. However, like most other aspects in life, we can sometimes have too much of a good thing, and crave some time to ourselves. Thus, we do not want either too much or too little social activity, but just what is individually right for any particular one of us.

7) Meaning in Life

For most of us, it is important to feel a connection with something larger than oneself. Although this may be linked to religion or spirituality, many also feel happy that they are part of a greater humanity and have a faith in the goodness of human nature. If we cannot see any meaning in our existence, then we will certainly not be happy. It is important that we are able to look back on a life lived so far, and be able to say that we have few regrets, and that we mostly did what we thought was right at the time. The humanistic psychologist Erik Erikson included this aspect in his criteria that contribute to what he called 'ego integrity' – a state of mind that should be achieved by all of us in later life.

Whatever our present age, it is equally important to be able to look forward, and to start to develop an understanding of our place in the universe. We need to use our minds to explore the spiritual gifts yet to come, however we may wish to define them. This topic was discussed in greater detail in the earlier article: 'The meaning of life'.

8) Freedom

In the United Kingdom, as in many other countries within the developed world, most people take personal freedom for granted. But in some lands many are oppressed, or so curtailed by poverty and autocratic regimes that they cannot even contemplate the freedom that we enjoy. Of course, even in our own country, freedom can be taken away from us if we break the law and are locked up in jail. There cannot have been a worse incarceration than being imprisoned in concentration camps like Auschwitz in the Second World War. Yet one of the inmates, Viktor Frankl, survived by always being able to find meaning in life no matter how terrible things were. He became a renowned psychologist of the humanistic school, and devised a therapeutic procedure called 'logo therapy', based on his own coping experiences.

9) Money

This 'dirty' word has been intentionally left until last. Did you include this in your happiness list? A question often asked is, "Can money bring happiness?" Much research has been done on this, and one conclusion is that it is not so much what we *have*, but how we *feel* about it. Whilst money itself might not be evil, the *love* of money is. Having too little of it to ensure survival certainly causes unhappiness but, once the poverty threshold has been crossed and we have a home, ample food, and clothing, then the joy gained from acquiring additional income is often short-lived. Indeed, the desire for more of it might just be prompted by a need to score over our neighbours!

Research carried out in the USA by Paul Piff and Jake Markowitz found that, as a general rule, wealthier people appear to take greater pleasure in their career achievements than do those who are less prosperous. In turn, poorer individuals usually value their friends and family more than do their richer associates. They also experience more awe and beauty in the world around them.

In the year two thousand and ten, Dr Chris Boyce of Warwick University wrote a piece about a married couple who won fifty-six million pounds on the National Lottery. He concluded that it would not make them happy. Why? Such wealth would change the couple's relationships with friends and neighbours, and probably result in a house move to a more up-market area where it might be difficult to fit in to the community. They would no doubt give up their jobs, and their daily routine would change. The outcome could well be that their lives would cease to have purpose; there would be little left to strive for. Buying expensive cars or boats would not remedy the situation.

Depression and despair was a likely outcome. Giving money away and engaging in voluntary work was the main advice Dr Boyce had to offer, but he added that this could still lead to arguments and family jealousies.

By coincidence, in November two thousand and seventeen there was an article in my newspaper about a syndicate of six ladies who worked as caterers in a Welsh hospital, that won over twenty-five million pounds on the lottery. They all resigned their jobs, presumably leaving the hospital department understaffed, and mentioned that they would spend money on such things as household items, a dream wedding and an overseas holiday. The piece ends by saying that the lucky winners were very emotional, "but very, very happy." It will be interesting to see if the time will come when Dr Boyce's comments will apply to them, and that being "very, very happy" will no longer apply.

Perhaps we can conclude by suggesting that there is no simple relationship between more money and more happiness. Having sufficient to be comfortable, and then trying to help others achieve the same standards, is a worthy goal, and there are many noteworthy philanthropists who have helped to enrich the lives of countless numbers of people who are worse of than themselves.

* * * * * * * * * * * * * *

So, can we summarise all these factors in one succinct formula to guide us along the path to everlasting happiness? I shall attempt to do so, but first it is important to take note of what Professor Simon Blackburn described as the 'Paradox of Hedonism'.

What this means is that the more you concentrate on happiness, then the more you worry about it, and the less likely you are to achieve it.

Thus don't try too hard, but here is my attempt at a happiness formula; once again note that the factors are not in any order of importance:

Money (enough to feel safe, warm, fed, and clothed)

PLUS

Health (sufficiently good health to be able to do pleasurable things)

PLUS

Activities (a range of pleasurable activities, and goals that are just right for you)

PLUS

Friends and family (sufficient to share love and social activities)

PLUS

Meaning (a belief that one's life is meaningful; an awareness of one's spiritual gifts; a recognition that there is a power greater than oneself)

PLUS

Freedom (free enough to be able to accomplish all of the above)

EQUALS
HAPPINESS!

(Note: Some passages in this chapter were previously published in my book 'Ageing Disgracefully, with Grace')

Chapter 13

Do you remember the war?

My late mother, Doris, was born in the year nineteen hundred and nine, in the district if Islington, London. Her father, Herbert, was a railway engineer employed by Crown Agents, and spent long periods of time working in West Africa.

Shortly after the commencement of World War One, German Zeppelin airships flew in to the UK over East Anglia. They could carry about two tons of bombs, and the first towns to suffer from the dropping of these were Great Yarmouth and King's Lynn in Norfolk. It was not long before these raids were concentrated on London itself. Official reports state that, in total, there were fifty-one such sorties during the war, resulting in five hundred and fifty-seven deaths and a further one thousand, three hundred and fifty-eight injured.

When I asked my mother about her earliest childhood recollections, she told me she remembered looking up and seeing these enormous airships flying overhead, but not making a sound that could be heard from the ground; it was all quite eerie. It seems that my grandfather Herbert was concerned for the safety of his wife, Emma, and their four young children, during his protracted absences abroad. He therefore decided to move the whole family away from the metropolis to an area of the country not subjected to the enemy bombing.

They first lived in a rented house in Lincoln, and remained there for the duration of the war, safely avoiding the dangers of the Zeppelins. Then, some time before nineteen thirty-six, Herbert bought the sixteenth century 'Ryland Manor' house, located in the village of Welton, six miles north of the city. This was a large, imposing dwelling, as befits its name, which had a few acres of land attached to it. In due course, each of the children married. Three of them moved away from home, including my mother, but the fourth continued to live in the house with his wife and their son.

The man who would become my father, Wilfred ('Bill') Lowis, was from Lincolnshire stock, being born in Dunston, about seven miles south of Lincoln. My parents married in the year nineteen thirty, in the church at Welton. Thus, if it had not been for the First World War and Herbert's desire to move the family away from

London to avoid the bombings, this romance would doubtless not have occurred, and I would not be writing this memoire.

Once he had retired, Grandfather Herbert developed the land attached to the Manor House into a smallholding, with chickens, ducks, and a few pigs. There was also an orchard, and one field was kept for growing crops. Grandmother Emma died in nineteen thirty-eight, almost a year before I was born, and Herbert passed away four years later. Unless my memory is deceiving me, I can just about recall some images of his swarthy figure wearing leather gaiters, stomping around his estate. My mother told me that he became very cross if any chicken dared to fly over the wire netting fence that surrounded their run. The unfortunate bird inevitably ended up on the kitchen table and then into the cooking pot.

My father was a journalist and, shortly after their marriage, the couple firstly moved to Surrey so he could take up an appointment as a reporter on a newspaper there. It was not long afterwards that he successfully applied for a more senior position on the *Huddersfield Examiner* in Yorkshire, which published an evening daily paper. There he and my mother remained until retirement, and it was where both my sister and I were born. Interestingly, the urge to return to their roots re-immerged in later life, and they bought a house in Lincolnshire close to where one of my mother's brothers lived.

I was born a month or two before the outbreak of World War Two, and the joke was often made that I was responsible for starting it! Because of his age, my father was only conscripted into the services – the Royal Air Force – in September, nineteen forty-one, which was two years after the war started. Like many others in the street where we lived, and the country as a whole, it was then left to the lady of the house to bring up the children by herself, and cope as best she could. It was not long before most homes were supplied with Morrison Shelters. These were free for families that earned less than £350 per year – the equivalent of about £21,600 at the time of writing (two thousand and seventeen).

The shelters had an oblong steel framework, nearly eight feet long, just over four and a half feet wide, and about three feet tall. The sides were of wire mesh, and one end opened like a gate. These were assembled in a downstairs room, and were usually disguised as a table by covering them with a cloth. When the air raid siren sounded, we all had to crawl into this cage and lie there until it was all clear again. One of my earliest memories is of entering our shelter with my mother, and hearing the enemy bombers overhead, along with our anti aircraft guns firing at them.

The siren itself was a clever invention, with a sound guaranteed to send shivers down the spine – a noise that certainly could not be ignored. In the UK, the design often comprised a pair of metal cylinders, with slots cut out of them, that rotated within similar outer casings. They could by cranked by hand or electrically powered. The sound they made was a discordant 'musical' minor third that undulated up and down in a characteristic way, like some mythical monster baying for blood. If anything reminds us of the war, it is this. These and similar devices are still used today as flood warnings and other pending catastrophes.

Some walk-in shelters were constructed on pieces of spare ground, for the benefit of people who were caught in the street when the siren sounded. These were oblong in shape, built of brick with flat, reinforced concrete roofs, and iron doors. After the war, children like me used to play in them. When the time came for them to be demolished, everybody seemed to help – including the kids.

Huddersfield was not a main target area; only one bomb was actually dropped on the town, and that was away from the main population. We somehow came into possession of a small curved piece of metal that was alleged to be part of the bomb casing. It was stored on the upper shelf of our mantelpiece for several years, until my mother threw it out. A pity, as it would have made an interesting souvenir all these years later.

It was a time of hardship for everyone, and a lonely one for me, especially before I started school. My sister, who was five years older than me, was at school. Father was away, of course, and mother always seemed to be busy. Food was rationed, and coal for the open fire was often in limited supply – no central heating for us in those days. I always seemed to be hungry or cold, or both. It helped if one 'knew a man who could fix you up', in other words obtain little luxuries on the 'black market'. Everybody seemed to be doing it, but a few eggs or an extra pack of butter now and again were useful supplements to a sometimes rather meagre diet.

A more legitimate way of obtaining more food was to grow it oneself. Allotments were provided for all who wanted them, and my family rented a small plot in what was originally the extensive garden of a posh house that had been partially demolished. The ruins that remained, and a small orchard behind them, provided plenty of scope for a young boy like me to explore and play whilst the adults were tending their vegetables. People were also encouraged to keep chickens, and my parents built a small run in the back garden for a few of these egg-producing machines. There was also an incentive to keep a pig or two. Although we did not avail ourselves of this opportunity, at least one family I knew did.

The occasions when father came home on leave were very special, and a time for rejoicing. He travelled back to Huddersfield by train, and then took a trolley bus for the almost two mile journey to the top of our street. When we knew of his estimated time of arrival, and I was old enough, I used to walk up the path alongside the road to meet him half way from the bus stop. These home visits were always too short, and it was so sad when he then had to retrace his steps to catch the bus back to the railway station.

The difficult times generated a good community spirit in our neighbourhood that it is hard to match in peacetime. Everyone supported and helped each other. Nothing was wasted. In fact it was a criminal offence to throw food away. People learned how to recycle materials to make and alter clothing rather than buy new garments, and they devised ways of adapting recipes and substituting ingredients for those that were unavailable, during their cooking and baking. The proverbial British 'stiff upper lip' prevailed, and we survived the hardships, grateful for what we had. Petty crime was low, and many people did not even lock their doors during the daytime.

What did help socially in our case was that my mother's elder sister and her husband lived in the same street as we did, only a short distance away from us. My uncle was a veteran from World War One, and had been wounded in the leg; his knee joint had been shattered, leaving it unable to bend it at all. Understandably, he was not conscripted for the armed services, so there was at least one adult male who was available to help when needed. They only had one child – a girl who was ten years older than I was, so she did not provide a playmate for me. In fact, until some years later, I cannot recall another boy of similar age living in the neighbourhood who could become a friend.

My father's service record reports that, after his basic training, he attended the service police training school, and later served in this capacity with the rank of acting corporal. A medical condition was then discovered that rendered him unsuitable for this role. Although the details are not stated, I suspect that the disability was a blindness that was starting to develop in one of his eyes. Now with the lower rank of leading aircraftman, he was allocated the role of 'general duties', which included anything from being a clerk to station guard.

On the first of April nineteen forty-two, he was posted to the Royal Air Force base at Pitreavie Castle, which is situated between Rosyth and Dunfermline in Scotland. This may seem to be an unusual sobriquet for a military establishment, but it was built under and around what was originally an early seventeenth century country house with this name. My dad said that the complex retained its moniker in order to confuse the Germans, who may have been looking for an airfield called Pitreavie. However, there was no aerodrome there.

Instead, this historic dwelling had been converted into a combined headquarters for both the Royal Navy and the Royal Air Force. Many outbuildings were added to house the personnel stationed there, but the key to this site was an elaborate, two-story underground command facility. This was divided into many rooms, including for sending and deciphering messages, weather forecasting, and planning maritime operations for almost the top half of the eastern United Kingdom coastline.

My mother took my sister and me on periodic visits to Scotland to see father. On at least one occasion this was for a long time, and my sister then went to the local school. We all stayed in a bed-sitting room and, to help keep the cost down, mother helped the landlady with her work, leaving me alone in the room upstairs. It was very lonely, and I was often frightened to be left on my own at the age of three or four. My father was sometimes able to join us in the lodgings, and at other times we went to the camp to see him. I have memories of being with him in one of the perimeter guard houses, and hiding from sight when a vehicle came to the gate to be admitted to the station.

Ever the journalist, my dad soon started a camp newspaper called 'The Pitreavie Post'. His superiors encouraged this as it helped moral and enabled other servicemen to contribute articles for publications. The very first copy was a simple, duplicated sheet but, once his efforts had been recognised, printing facilities were made available to him and the resulting editions were quite professional.

My father's service record states that he attended hospital on two occasions during this time, each for a duration of nineteen days, but the reasons are not stated. However, it was obviously serious enough for him to be discharged before the war ended. This was in July, nineteen forty-four, and the reason given was: "Below Air Force physical standard." We were indeed fortunate to have the family back together again, when for so many people this happened much later, or not at all. He resumed his journalist job, but he also joined the local Air Raid Wardens for the duration of the conflict, which entailed working shifts through the night.

During our visits to see him when he was stationed at Pitreavie, we travelled by steam train. This was a long and boring journey, especially for young children, but I was always told to look out of the window when the train crossed over the famous Forth Bridge. The massive slanting steel girders that formed the framework of this structure flashed past the window, creating a characteristic zigzag pattern. Once across the estuary, we knew that our final destination was not too far away.

Another memory of this time in Scotland was visits to the seaside resort of Aberdour, just seven miles to the east of the camp site. During the summer it was a chance to play on the sand and paddle in the sea, which is just what children like to do, even during a war. Somewhere in this area there was a large park, where we were taken to see parades of Scottish soldiers marching in their colourful kilts to the stirring sound of drums and bagpipes. They then lay down and used rifles to engage in some target practice. However, I don't think that live ammunition was used, but what looked like a small metal rod popped out of the end of the barrel when the trigger was pulled. It only travelled a few feet, and could be retrieved and used again.

In addition to these occasional visits to Scotland, during the nineteen forties and early fifties my mother, sister and I made many trips to the Manor House in Lincoln, and it was a happy place for a town-dwelling boy to be. There were chickens and ducks to feed, eggs to collect, a pigsty to muck out, and an orchard plus, some arable land where vegetables were growing.

Whether my efforts were a hindrance or a help remains debatable, but for me it was a lot of fun. The family tried to be as self-sufficient as possible, and were also able to sell their surplus produce on a stall at Lincoln market.

It is ironic that my mother's side of the family moved to Lincolnshire to escape World War One, and ended up being surrounded by many airfields during World War Two. One that became famous was only a short bicycle ride away: Scampton, the home of the Dam Busters squadron. Bombers took off most nights, and it was the practice of people to look up and count the number of planes as they set out on their raid, and then again as they returned. The numbers were rarely the same and, sadly, nationally about half of the aircrew of Bomber Command were either killed, wounded, or taken prisoner over the course of the war.

At last, in May, 1945 the war in Europe mercifully came to an end. This must have been anticipated, because I remember sitting next to the radio with the rest of the family, waiting for the formal announcement. When it came, what joy and relief this must have generated for millions of people – much more than a six-year-old boy like me could have appreciated. The final act of the war, the surrender of Japan, followed in September of the same year.

At least one of these events was celebrated by a large, communal bonfire near where we lived, along with some fireworks that must have been saved from before the war. This was the first time for many years that fires and lights were permitted outside at night, due to the total blackout that had been in force to avoid revealing evidence of habitation to the enemy bombers. The traditional November the fifth celebrations followed later, and of course it was the first one for me. These events were so enjoyable that Guy Fawkes night has been one of my favourite times of the year ever since.

At least one prisoner of war camp was built near Huddersfield. During one of his leave periods my father took me on a walk into the hills to see a camp. I can just recall the sight of a few dispirited-looking men milling about behind the perimeter fence. Later, when the war was over, and dad had resumed his journalistic career, we often went on the same walk and visited the same camp, now abandoned like a ghost town. It was eventually demolished, but it seemed to a young lad like me that many sad memories were circulating like a wind through these empty huts and many more like them, on both sides of the conflict. What a waste; what sadness and tragic losses occurred over those five years of warring. Does anyone actually win a war?

Chapter 14

The 'third age': Activity or disengagement?

At what stage of life are people considered to be in their 'third age'? There can be no hard cut-off point, but it is generally considered to commence on retirement from a full-time job, and end when physical and mental constraints unacceptably interfere with desirable activities. Whilst the ages sixty-five to eighty might be a typical span, these golden years can be extended if we suitably modify our aims and ambitions when some of the more demanding ones become impractical.

Researchers have devised several different models of ageing, in an attempt to determine which sort of life-style is likely to lead to the greatest satisfaction. However, it would be surprising if there was only one model or theory that applied to every person and every circumstance. Here is a brief summary of them, so that you the reader can decide which you think is the most appropriate for your own situation. We start with the two that appear to convey completely opposing messages.

'Disengagement Theory' dates back to nineteen sixty-one, when Elaine Cumming and William Henry concluded that ageing involves an inevitable withdrawal or disengagement process. This results in a decreased interaction between an individual and other people. The change can be initiated either by the person concerned, or by others, and can occur in three ways. There can be a decrease in the number of contacts, a change in the style or pattern of interaction, or an increased preoccupation with oneself. It is as if society as a whole, and the individual, are equally programmed to allow this to take place.

The researchers suggested that one or all of these can be triggered by loss of family and friends, ill health and deteriorating ability, or a preoccupation with the past. Indeed, there is an air of inevitability about the whole disengagement syndrome. Despite such negative connotations, the process is often found to be equally satisfying both for the people concerned, and those around them. However, not all commentators agree with this conclusion, maintaining instead that the change was not welcome, and the withdrawal was linked to lack of opportunities for this age group.

In contrast, the principles underpinning 'Activity Theory' were first voiced in the year nineteen fifty-three by Robert Havighurst and Ruth Albrecht. These researchers concluded from the results of a large-scale survey, that the more active older people are, then the better they adjusted they are. Others agreed, adding that such individuals tended to be interested in productive hobbies and manual pursuits.

It is important to find activities to replace those lost on retirement, not only the ones relating to achievements and productivity, but also to the contact we have with other people. Being active does not just mean doing something physical all the time, and it would be unrealistic to expect older people to maintain the same energy level as they had when younger. Those who have studied this model have concluded that there are three groups of activities: the informal (social interaction with friends), the formal (the same, but as a member of formal organisations), and the solitary (reading and hobbies.

Is it possible to come to a definite conclusion about which of these two theories is correct? Many factors will influence how people cope when they reach the third age, and often there will be environmental constraints that inhibit the direction in which their natural inclination is pointing. It is probably a case of comparing what the individual would like to do, with what society will allow them to do, coupled with what he or she is actually capable of doing. We all look forward to a happy and meaningful retirement, and try to prepare ourselves for the day when this will occur, but are we being realistic, and does the 'system' allow us to follow our chosen pathway?

There are two additional models of ageing that are worth a mention, and they may help to resolve the dilemma. The first is called 'Continuity Theory' and, like the others already discussed, it dates back quite a long way. In nineteen sixty-two, Suzanne Reichard and her colleagues noted that there were many different ways of adjusting to retirement. They concluded that the best-adjusted people were those who were able to develop a life-style that provided continuity with the past, and also met long-term needs. Even those who may be classed as 'disengaging' or 'active' using the criteria of the theories already discussed were, in reality, continuing an earlier life-style.

Others have made a distinction between 'internal continuity' – maintaining a sense of identity, self-esteem, integrity, and a way of interacting with others, and 'external continuity' – preserving relationships and roles within the circle of family and friends. Continuity also implies maintaining goals, and continuing to use the expertise that one has developed over the preceding years. However, it may be that being able to continue doing things that are satisfying for an individual's personality, is more important than the type of activity per se. For example, extraverts are likely to be motivated by different activities than are introverts.

But what of those who say, "When I retire, I am going to emigrate, explore new lands, adopt a completely new life-style." These people are regarded as maintaining what psychologists call a 'risk-taking personality', and it is within their nature to seek out, and adapt to, new ways of life at any age. Thus, it is still a case of continuity, but a continuity that thrives on change.

The final model is called 'Selectivity Theory', which is more recent than the others, being proposed by Laura Carstensen in the nineteen-nineties. It is intended to account for the changes in social contact that accompany ageing. Whilst some forms of interaction may decrease during the later part of the lifespan, perhaps due to retirement, dispersal, or death of friends and family, others are maintained. What is important is the purpose and quality of the relationships that are retained.

It is suggested that we become more selective as we grow older, although this is not the same as withdrawal. The emotional aspect of our social contacts increases in importance as we age, but not all interactions are important. Thus, we tend to select the types of relationships that are the most likely to lead to positive feelings, with quality being more important than quantity.

So there we have the varying views of those who have investigated the topic of what is likely to lead to a satisfying life in the third age. Do any of these make sense to you, especially if you are already in this group? In the earlier article, 'Ageing Disgracefully', examples were given of individuals who had achieved great things in their later years, such as composing music, winning sporting trophies, and being awarded university degrees. Whilst most of us may struggle to reach such dizzy heights, we can all still enjoy striving for realistic but challenging goals after we have retired from full-time work.

As a research psychologist, some years ago I decided to do some studies of my own. A survey was carried out on a large sample of retired men, in order to try and uncover evidence that would either support or oppose the two main models of ageing. Participants firstly completed a questionnaire to measure their current level of life satisfaction, and they then rated a large number of factors that could contribute toward it. The greatest support was for the Activity Theory: those who had the highest life satisfaction scores were the most content with their daily activities, social contacts, and family involvement. They were also the most likely to participate in voluntary associations.

Does this mean that the Disengagement Theory has no credibility? The answer is 'no'. With all social science research like this, no result is one hundred percent valid, just as no two people are completely alike. The findings will be heavily influenced by who was surveyed, the specific questions that were asked, and how much variation there was in the scores across the whole group. Quoting only the average results ignores individual differences, and gives a false impression that all people are the same. Good researchers always include a statement that details the range of scores that was obtained.

The popularity of the notion that we disengage from society in later life might have now waned somewhat, as the more recent emphasis has been on remaining as active as possible. However, having now entered the third age myself, it is becoming increasingly evident that at least some degree of disengagement is inevitable. This, despite having so many tasks to complete that it is rare to be able to accomplish them all within the same day. Or, could it be just that it takes longer than it used to do to achieve a relatively small number of things, thus giving the impression that life is a continuous hive of activity?

Have you noticed how older people like to talk about the past? It is easy to think that this is because the elderly have little to interest them in the present, and even less to look forward to in the future. This is a rather cynical view. Sometimes it is good to let younger friends and relatives know what it was like before the latest technology came along, and to learn something about their family history. This backward look can be therapeutic, and it comes in two forms: life review, and reminiscence.   .

These may seem to be similar concepts, but 'reminiscence' involves telling stories about your past life, and revealing specific events that are significant for you. The re-telling of these anecdotes can serve several purposes, including enhancing self-esteem and self-worth, confirming self-identity, encouraging and enriching social exchanges, transmitting cultural heritage, and simply providing enjoyment for the teller.

Another use is to provide material for 'life review' which, in contrast to simple story telling, is a personal and intense process, representing an active grappling with the past in order to come to terms with it. Older people are apt to review their lives on the basis of their original intentions and potentials, and thereby conclude that they have fulfilled or failed themselves now that they are in a position to experience life as a whole.

So important is this that some clinical psychologists use 'Life Review Therapy' to help their older clients. The therapist asks him or her to construct an autobiography, perhaps using family albums, letters and interviews, to gain information about behaviour and emotions at crucial points in their life. This can then help the person to explore feelings such as guilt, fear and unfulfilled ambitions, and assist him or her to work through these outstanding issues. Whilst this can be beneficial, such a process can also possibly raise anxiety and feelings of depression over what might be perceived as a wasted life.

My own research on this topic indicated that those people who were still in the process of reviewing their lives often had negative feeling about themselves. However, the ones who had completed the review and were no longer spending time revisiting their past, seemed to have come to terms with whatever they had said and done, and were much more positive, with a higher self-esteem. It therefore seems that undertaking such a review is an essential task of later life. To an onlooker, it may appear that a person who is going through this process is becoming too introspective and disengaged but, for the individual concerned, it is just a journey that will eventually be completed.

How can we resolve the seemingly opposing theories of activity versus disengagement, not forgetting the continuity and selectivity models? Each of these ideas came from studies that were conducted by experienced researchers, and each was supported by a statistical analysis of survey data. Like many apparent conflicts in life, the answer will be something of a compromise. Each view has something to contribute, and will reflect the situation with at least some people for some of the time.

We all need meaningful goals at any age, so that when we wake up in the morning we have things to do and challenges to be met, otherwise life will not have any meaning. Activities are, therefore, important but this does not mean trying to continue at the same rate we may have done when we were younger. Recall what was stated earlier: it is not the quantity of activities that is important, but the quality – it must be what is right for the individual. Although this may imply continuity, continuing with what you a familiar, it will also require selectivity.

Some activities will cease to be practical due to both internal and external constraints. We therefore need to be realistic, and select what is feasible, whilst at the same time not be afraid to try something new. The brain continues to be capable of learning throughout its life, even though it may take a little longer than it used to do. There are many opportunities 'out there' for all ages, including lifelong learning.

But then we all need a quiet time to relax and reflect on our life, and this is where the disengagement theory has validity. Maybe our hearing or vision is not as good as it used to be, and that makes it difficult for us to join in some activities, even if the desire is there. There will always be a youth culture with different music, technology and ways of behaving that leaves older people feeling like foreigners in their own country.

At other times, however, it is pleasurable when folk of all ages come together for a common cause, or an occasion like a family gathering. But it has been said many times that it is so nice to have parties for children and grandchildren where everyone has a jolly time, but it also quite a relief when they have all gone home!

As the inevitable march of time continues, the need for peace and quite, and time for reflection, may increase, but the need to retain some goals and activities never ceases. It is simply a case of finding the correct balance between activity and disengagement.

Chapter 15

Bosses I have worked for

Some people manage to stay with the same employer for their whole working career, even if their role changes through internal transfers or promotion. This steady income and financial stability will usually allow them to be free of a home mortgage millstone round their necks many years before retirement, as well as accumulate a maximum pension entitlement. Many more will have worked for just two or three different organisations, enjoying a varied career and, hopefully, an advance in seniority with each successive move. Yet others, but probably a minority, will have chopped and changed many more times – perhaps too many. They will have had an interesting and varied, but at times unstable employment history, and then reached retirement age with a limited pension and a house that was still not fully paid for.

My working life falls into the latter category. I had six employers before we emigrated in nineteen seventy-five, seven whilst in South Africa, and one full-time plus two part-time jobs on my return to the United Kingdom twenty years later. Any regrets? Only that my departure from four of the positions overseas was not voluntary! Job security out there, and labour law that would protect workers, were both virtually non-existent. It was a 'hire and fire' environment. In case you are wondering, there are no proverbial skeletons in my cupboard that will reveal any misdemeanours of mine, and my conscience is clear. However, all these goings-on are part of another story (see my book *Twenty Years in South Africa – an Immigrant's Tale*).

The memory of each of the bosses for whom I worked remains with me. The first one was in charge of a small hospital laboratory where, straight from grammar school at the tender age of sixteen, I was training to be a technician. He was an elderly (or so he seemed to me) Scotsman, married to an Irish woman who worked in the same lab as a cleaner. Between them they had some amusing turns of phrase, such as: "I should have went to the shops". At first he seemed supportive and father-like to a raw lad like me, but the relationship eventually became strained. I am not sure why now, but I probably became somewhat rebellious during my progression through the teenage years. After four years, and the completion of the first part of my training, it was time to move on.

My next job was with a Public health Laboratory in a nearby town. The Chief Technician there was an ex-military man who ran the place rather formally, although fairly, in a style that he would have used during his time in the services. He lived with his wife in a flat on the top floor of the building, and a more human side of him emerged when he revealed he was a pianist. As I played the saxophone (and still do) he invited me upstairs to join him for a few jazzy duets during the lunch breaks. After two years, and with my final examinations successfully passed, the opportunity to earn a more realistic salary as a fully qualified technician beckoned.

Back in my home town, the local Public Health Department had a small lab staffed by just a single technician. The position was currently vacant, and I successfully applied for it. Now this was a very different scenario. There were no experienced colleagues to help, and the incumbent nominally reported to one or more of the medical doctors there. These were predominantly occupied with their own duties, as well as being understandably less trained in the finer details of laboratory work than would be any qualified technician. Working there, especially without the constant intervention of a boss, was challenging but enjoyable, and I became quite friendly with one of young doctors for whom public health work was a new experience.

It would have been easy to have lingered on in this environment, but one-man departments do not leave much scope for promotion. With this being a local government position, pay scales and other conditions of service were fixed. I was about to be married, and needed the opportunity to advance on merit. A job in the private sector would surely be the answer, as the opportunities for growth and advancement would no doubt be limitless, and budgets would be flexible – or so I thought. This might be the case with some companies, but not with the large pharmaceuticals conglomerate I joined. It was so large that it had to have as many restrictive policies and procedures as would any government department.

Locating to another town with my new wife, and trying to find an affordable house to buy, whilst on a salary scale just one increment ahead of the previous one, was tough. Only a very understanding bank manager who allowed me to be constantly overdrawn saved us from the debtors' prison. My job was in a very small sub-unit within an extensive suite of laboratories. The immediate boss was a decent man, but everything was so formal that, throughout my three years there, no first names were used between us. He was answerable to a superior who was in charge of three of the sub-units, and had his own small office, whereas my boss shared his with two others, and I only had a desk in the lab itself. In turn, the boss's boss reported to a manager who had more departments and a larger office. Do you get the picture? It was all prescribed in black and white. Come back Civil Service, all is forgiven!

Once again it became obvious that the chances of an upward move were nil, and it was thus necessary to move on. A new position with a food manufacture was advertised, and it was within travelling distance of home. The company was about to make their first perishable product, and they needed somebody to set up and run a microbiology laboratory for quality control purposes. Fortunately, my application was accepted.

All went well at first, with a corporate technical boss and a local managing director, neither of whom bothered me much. But then the empire-building began.

The MD appointed a deputy, and my position was placed under him. Again there was little interference, but then another intermediary was appointed further down the hierarchy, and I had to report to that incumbent. There was now more interference. The company was then taken over by a large conglomerate, and it sent its own person to take overall responsibility for microbiology. Oh dear, job satisfaction plummeted. It was time to search through the situations vacant pages yet again.

After fifteen years in a laboratory-based job, my sixth appointment was in a managerial position at a food manufacturer near my home town. My portfolio of responsibilities embraced factory hygiene, safety and security. Not only was this a different category of work, but it required managing and organising about two dozen subordinates. Have you heard of the 'Peter Principle'? It was a theory formulated by Laurence J. Peter in nineteen sixty-nine, which states that people are promoted until they reach their level of incompetence. Was this going to happen to me who, up until then, had only been responsible for a single assistant, not a whole department?

Fortunately, the parent company had a training officer who periodically visited the manufacturing units to present courses on leadership and management. The knowledge that there were actual techniques in these functions was a revelation that was to influence the rest of my working career. So it was not, after all, only a case of learning by one's mistakes and upsetting many people along the way. Although my position reported to an intermediary, the factory manager was an interesting character who could be understanding and considerate one day, and vindictive the next.

The volatile mood of this man may have been partly due to his very painful back problem that sometimes flared up, but it was no doubt also influenced by his own officious superior who made regular visits to the factory. If this man said "jump", then you very obediently touched your forelock and jumped.

There was a sideways move for me during my five years at this factory. Although the work was satisfying, it was clear that there would be little chance of advancement to a higher level in the foreseeable future. In the nineteen seventies, the British economy was in a period of recession. There was double-digit inflation, and strikes were frequent – especially by the coal miners. Much of industry was forced to work a three-day week in order to conserve power.

It was time to think hard about my career, and the quality of life that my wife and young family deserved. Surely there should be something better than this. The only answer seemed to be emigration to a country with a growing economy and an available labour force, where technical skills were needed. With some sadness for what we would leave behind, but a feeling of excitement for the new life ahead of us, in nineteen seventy-five we set sail for South Africa.

If the bosses in Britain generally tried to do an honest and fair job, underpinned by a company personnel policy that in turn reflected government employment and labour laws, it would soon become clear that this was not to be the case in our adopted country. And neither were there any unemployment benefits for those out of work. Before leaving the UK, I had written to a food company in South Africa. They asked me to contact them on arrival there, which I did, and was offered a job at one of their units located about twenty miles east of Johannesburg. The factory manager had obviously received orders from his superior, as he had no choice in my recruitment. It was not long before he disappeared, to be replaced by his superior's son.

The young man was a little out of his depth, but was obviously being propped up by his dad. Things went well for me at first, but soured when a promised salary review yielded no increase. There was no obvious problem with my work, and the explanation was that a 'review' meant just that, rather than an automatic increase. Whilst this may have been semantically correct, it was not what was expected. My protests to the group personnel manager resulted in me being summoned to the office of the rather green factory manager. He told me that he had received instructions to dismiss me. I should have learned from this, but was slow to catch on.

Fortunately, I had already been putting out feelers for another job, and quickly obtained a position with a large pharmaceuticals manufacturing company on the south-western side of Johannesburg. My boss was a complete gentleman, and a delight to work for. However, after about two years, and for reasons never disclosed, he left the company. To my surprise, he was replaced by me. As is usually the case with pharmaceuticals companies, this one had plenty of money. Every level from superintendent upwards was provided with a car, with the make and model dependent on status. As you moved up through the ranks, you were obliged to immediately upgrade your vehicle.

The managing director had a way of operating that, I suspect, drew heavily on his religious and brotherhood affiliations, neither of which applied to me. You were either in favour, or you were out. At first I was 'in', but then the day came when I was 'out', having been called to his office just as everyone else was going home, and told not to come in the next day. This came completely without warning, and I nearly had a nervous breakdown when it happened.

Ah well, life must go on, and my next stop was a cosmetic and toiletries company, at a lower position but still managerial and with car. History was repeating itself. My first boss was a very kind and considerate man, but he seemed to have difficulty keeping up with his work. Before very long, he was 'moved on', and replaced by somebody more efficient but less likeable. After nearly three years, the company made several people redundant, including me. This was becoming the norm rather than the exception!

Back to the food industry now, and answerable to the site manager. He had his favourites, which presumably included me – at first. All seemed to be going well, but the boss was very ambitious. He talked his superiors into letting him take over his main competitor, and then raised the prices of the products. Now, with a monopoly, he wrongly thought that the supermarkets would have no alternative but to pay more. Instead, they all boycotted both brand names, and he was eventually forced to climb down with a great loss of face.

A condition of the take-over was that a senior member of the competitor's staff would join the company, and my function was placed under him. Unfortunately, his home country had been on the other side during the two World Wars, and he still seemed to resent being on the losing side. It was only a matter of time before the call came for me to: "Please come to my office. We have never got on well", he said. "Here is your termination letter and cheque for a month's salary. Go now."

Five months of unemployment followed, which was a tad worrying in a country with no social benefit system. Eventually, a position was found at a local food manufacturing company, answerable to the factory manager. As was the case with my first job in that country, he had not been consulted on my appointment, and seemed resentful and suspicious, often omitting to pass on important information. The job level was lower than ideal, and therefore an eye was kept on the situations vacant columns. After less than six months, I handed in my resignation (voluntarily this time!) and went to work for a large packaging company at a more appropriate level of employment.

My boss was the senior manager on site, and one of the most interesting characters to whom I have reported in my long and varied career. He was an ex rugby player, and his first language was Afrikaans. Although his English was quite acceptable, he had a quaint way of corrupting certain well known expressions. These were usually rude, and it would be inappropriate to reproduce them here. However, whilst we might say, "Get your finger out!" in order to motivate someone, he would reverse this and direct the individual concerned to remove the part of the anatomy that was metaphorically enveloping one's finger. When he thought somebody was speaking nonsense, whereas we might proclaim that it was a waste product from *either* a bull, *or* horse, he would combine the two animals in his unique version.

Numerous swear words peppered most of his conversations, but only when the audience was male. If he did not like the wine we had at corporate functions, he would say to all within earshot that it was "battery acid!" This expression is still used in my home today, even though we have no idea what battery acid actually tastes like.

This man was very direct, tolerated no nonsense, and you always knew whether you had done well or badly. If the latter, you entered his office in fear and trepidation, and left it shaking after his 'straight to the point' admonishment. Nevertheless, he appreciated hard and honest work from his staff, and was always ready to help if asked. Many did not like his style, but it suited me, and everything seemed to be going well. Why do good times never last? The boss was upgraded to a position at the corporate head office, and was replaced by a man who had modern ideas, but also a desire to build his personal empire.

For third time in my working life, my function – quality assurance – was placed under an intermediary boss. This was not very successful (the 'Peter Principle' was operating strongly with the individual concerned), so a new person was brought in. After a time, he too appointed an intermediary, and I now reported to him. Job satisfaction, already on a downward slope, rapidly plummeted. Job vacancies were again scrutinised. This soon resulted in my final job whilst living overseas, again with a packaging manufacturer, and answerable to another most interesting character.

He was the founder and outright owner of the company, having started with a plastics moulding machine in his garage, and expanding to a workforce of over fifty, which could increase during busy times. At staff level there was a production manager, me who looked after quality and human resources, an order clerk, and two office ladies. A very lean team, with no time wasted on meetings because the boss/founder/owner took all the big decisions. Whilst this may seem, and indeed was, an autocratic way to run a business, it was very efficient and everyone knew exactly where they stood at all times. Even at my level, if you had to take an hour off to go to the doctor or dentist, then you worked an extra hour to make up for it.

Whilst there were times when I hated the boss for his hard behaviour, he showed that he also had a soft side. The day I left to prepare for my return to the UK, he called me into his office and passed me an envelope saying "Here is a little bonus for you." When I opened it, it was stuffed with fifty pound notes! The foreign exchange situation was quite restrictive, and I don't know how he managed to acquire so much British currency, but I was not complaining. Now, about twenty years later, it was a pleasure to be able to locate him again and exchange some email messages.

For thirteen of our twenty years in South Africa, I had pursued part-time study in order to build on the in-house leadership courses run by my last employer in the UK. By the time we returned, I was a qualified psychologist with a desire to teach this subject at university. After a term of temporary appointment at one college, a full-time position became available nearer home, and there I remained until retirement. It was satisfying but demanding work, and helping to educate the next generation was a suitable culmination to a very varied career.

The departmental boss was a woman who tried to do everything correctly, generate a budget surplus, and generally impress her superiors. The day-to-day organising of lecturing schedules and other duties was left to an intermediary, also female, who was arguably the best leader I have encountered. As it happened, all my previous superiors had been male, so it was a new experience for me. She was very approachable and helpful, and fully aware that I was on a steep learning curve in what was a new environment for me. However, if a mistake was made, you were left in no doubt about it, but were not made to feel resentful. For my sins, I was sent on an in-house course on political correctness, to try and banish the blokeish approach I must have portrayed, formed due to many years of male-dominated work relationships.

The significant contribution that this person made was clearly not recognised by her superiors, and she was obliged to seek promotion at another institution. This was a great loss to the department. She was so popular that two or three other lecturers went to work for her at her new university. Her replacement was a man who was a reasonable person, but not in the same league as his predecessor.

So there we have it, fourteen full-time jobs and, including the additional managers that were brought in to intermediate positions, seventeen bosses. Some were devious and objectionable, other were neutral, but the last three stand out as being special in their individual ways: the ex rugby player, the founder/owner of the plastics company, and the woman who guided me in my lecturing job in the UK. The only boss I have now is my wife!

Chapter 16

Why music?

It was mentioned in an earlier article that music had the power to trigger profound emotional experiences known as 'peaks'. I stated that it is a special form of non-verbal communication that appeals directly to the 'soul', and it forms a bridge to the inner, spiritual world. Does this sound too fanciful? If you are one of those who are not passionate about music, or are content to just have it playing in the background whilst you are doing something else, then you may think that it is an over-statement –   and you might be right!

In this chapter, more details will be given on the history of music, before then discussing a novel method for conducting research on 'slippery' topics such as artistic appreciation, religion, or spirituality. The importance of conducting research in a proper manner has been mentioned several times already in this book. It is commonly referred to as the 'scientific method'. In order to avoid bias, and just collect data to support the view that you may already hold, it is essential to conduct experiments in such a way that there is an equal chance of proving or disproving what you seeking. Once data have been collected, a statistical analysis of the findings should then be used to reveal the probability (or not) that your initial claim has been supported.

This system works very well for studies that involve the hard sciences like physics and chemistry. It is also particularly useful for the social sciences such as psychology, in order to avoid false claims. To take just a simple example, say you were interested in seeing if children who play violent computer games exhibit higher levels of aggressive behaviour than do those who don't play them. You could study this by firstly assessing the existing aggression levels of on a large sample of children of similar age, and then randomly dividing them into two groups. One group would spend time playing the computer games, whilst the other one would use the computer for a non-violent purpose.

Afterwards, you would repeat the aggression test on all the children, and then statistically analyse the difference in scores between the two groups. There would either be a significant difference, in which case you could claim your idea had been supported, or not. If the latter, you would have to think again.

This works well when 'hard' data can be collected, but suppose you were interested to find out if music was just an innate gift for our enjoyment, or that it had survival value and was therefore the product of evolutionary development. Such an investigation leaves little scope for collecting test scores and following the scientific method. Questions like these should not be avoided just because of this limitation, and I was keen to study this for myself. It was obvious that a novel type of methodology was called for.

Firstly, however, let us look in more detail at the origins of music. But before we can proceed any further, we need to define just what it is. Sound originates from waves of compression and decompression in the air, caused by an object vibrating. Musical sound was stated by the renowned conductor and composer Leonard Bernstein, as being structured into time and space, forming the components of melody, rhythm, tone colour (timbre), and harmony. This last feature is based on a universal known as the harmonic series, first described by Pythagoras about five hundred years before the Christian Era (BCE), following his discovery that a plucked string produces progressively higher notes as it is shortened.

Music has certainly been around since the dawn of history. What is believed to be part of a bone flute was found to be from forty-three thousand to sixty-seven thousand years old. It was thus made at a time when Neanderthals still roamed the earth. Later, and more obvious, flute specimens have been dated to twenty-seven thousand BCE, only four thousand years after Homo sapiens first appeared. King Shulgi of Sumaria, who lived in the twenty-second century BCE, claims to have established the theory of music and instrumentation. The oldest known examples of a noted melody are those for the lyre or harp that originated in Babylon around twelve hundred years before Christ, but they are difficult to interpret now.

Researchers speculate that our early ancestors will have heard the 'musical' noises of nature – such as the wind blowing through reeds, the sonorous tone of an object hitting a hollow log, and the vocalisations of animals or birds. Perhaps they tried to mimic such sounds or, independent of this, came to produce sing-song noises through the rise, fall, and drawing out of their own utterances, particularly when expressing emotions or exhibiting sexual display. As stated in the earlier article, music may even have pre-dated speech, having started as crooning noises made by mothers to their babies to help foster emotional bonding between them.

Having now filled in some details about the topic of interest, we can return to the matter of how we can conduct research on quite a profound question, namely: is music an innate gift, perhaps even a divine one if you subscribe to such ideas, for our enjoyment, or is it the product of evolutionary development because it has survival value?

The procedure adopted to investigate this was not to conduct experiments myself, but to use deductive reasoning through a series of arguments that lead to logically valid conclusions. This may seem complicated but, in really, it is not so please bear with me for a while longer. One needs to start with a statement, or premise. For the present exercise, I decided upon: "Musical appreciation is an innate gift." The next step is to try and shoot this down by pitching it against a counter-argument, and seek evidence to support it. If the original premise survives this challenge, its validity is strengthened, although not proved, and it is ready to face another opponent.

The more times it emerges the victor from such challenges, then the more likely it is to be correct. However, it cannot be claimed that the statement has been 'proven beyond any doubt', but just that is more likely to be correct the more times it overcomes the opposition. There is always the chance that, some time in the future, a successful challenger may come along. If it falls in the face of any of the counter-arguments, then it is time to bury the idea and think again.

Although any conclusion reached from this multi-stage exercise will not be as strong as those obtained through the scientific method with statistical analyses, what is known as 'the weight of accumulated evidence' can lead to a high probability that it is true. We all probably use this principle without realising it. To take just a simple example, we may have to eat a particular food item on three separate occasions before it dawns on us that it was responsible for the heartburn that developed an hour or two later. There comes a time when we realise it was not just a coincidence.

For the current topic, two main counters come to mind to oppose the notion that music is an innate gift:

firstly that it is learned and, secondly, that it is the product of evolution. In order to explore these, therefore, we can lead off with the first argument:

If all aspects of musical appreciation (the ability to process and enjoy music) are learned (culturally acquired), then it cannot be an innate gift.

What evidence is there that enjoyment of music is something that has to be learned? Some researchers do claim that it is indeed culturally acquired, and this is why people in different countries enjoy different kinds of music. For example, Japanese or Indian songs use notes that may sound out of tune to Western ears, and vice versa. People learn what is performed in their native lands from their parents and peers, and come to accept and enjoy it. Studies have shown that babies can hear music whilst still in the womb, and can even respond to it if it is relayed through a speaker placed on the mother's abdomen.

But there is also evidence that not everything about music is learned. Experiments with children as young as one to five days have shown that some listening skills are present at birth. In particular, the babies were able to tell the difference between 'pleasing' and 'discordant' harmonies, as indicated by their physical reactions when such examples were played to them. By the age of four months, the infants turned their heads toward the 'good' sounds, and away from the 'bad'. At the age of eight months, they were found to actually be superior to adults in being able to detect melodic changes within the same key signature. This occurred even when songs from other countries were played to them, which would not have been previously heard by either mother or child.

Those who have conducted many studies of this type have come to the conclusion that infants have an innate preference for pleasing melodies, and that this is even reflected in the 'musical' babblings of pre-lingual children. One team of researchers stated that their experiments showed that music plays a special role among the higher brain functions, as it is universally appreciated even at birth.

Based on evidence such as this, the first argument can be resolved thus:

Not all musical appreciation is learned, therefore at least some musical abilities are inherent.

Thus, the original premise has survived the first challenge, and is now ready to face the next.

If not all aspects of music appreciation can be attributed to social learning, then did this ability develop because it had an evolutionary advantage, and help our species to survive and advance? This possibility can be explored through seeking support for the second argument:

If at least some aspects of musical appreciation are inherent, then music always has survival value, or it is an innate gift for our aesthetic enjoyment.

The views of scholars who have studied this topic are mixed. Some claim that there are biological roots to art, and that its purpose is to transmit information, including emotion. For music, the evidence includes the universal practice of singing lullabies to babies, as has been mentioned already. Even when the words are filtered out, this form of music can be recognised from its repetitive nature, and by being soothing, soft, simple, and slow. Children as young as thirty-five months have been found to modify their own singing voices when in the presence of infant siblings.

Although the use of music to foster emotional bonding may suggest that the claim of it being an innate gift for our enjoyment is not supported, it is now necessary to turn to aesthetic considerations. Sandra

Trehub, working with various collaborators, is probably the person who has carried out the most extensive research on music and babies. It is significant that, from her many studies, she concluded that the relative ease with which infants process simple-ratio melodies and harmonies, 'is a basic and uniquely human disposition – one that is not related to acquired knowledge or utility.' In other words, it is an innate disposition.

The human ear has the ability to detect sounds, including musical ones, of frequencies up to about 12 kHz, which is far higher than the top note of the piano or any other instrument. This is not something that has to be learned, and there seems to be no current explanation for why we possess it. However, audible high notes played or sung appear to bypass all perceptual and cognitive mechanisms, and appeal directly to the very 'soul'.

Music certainly gives pleasure to all but a few individuals. The Group for the Advancement of Psychiatry opined that aesthetic reactions touched off by music and other art forms are characterised by a change in the sense of reality, in which the external world is distorted or excluded. Music can cause strong physical as well as emotional responses. One term that has been used to summarise these is 'tingles', which can include shivers, laughter, and tears.

How, therefore, might the second argument be resolved? Does the notion of the survival value of lullabies outweigh the fact that preference for harmonious music, even in babies, does not seem to be related to acquired knowledge or utility? How much credence should be afforded to the aesthetic qualities of this art form, which can generate tingles of delight or 'peak emotional experiences'? It is difficult to explain all these aspects in terms of survival factors alone. The suggested resolution is, therefore, as follows:

Music does not always have survival value, therefore some aspects of musical appreciation are a gift for our aesthetic enjoyment.

The conclusion thus far, based on the first two challenges, is that the weight of evidence points toward music being a gift for our enjoyment. However, the process could, and should, be continued with the premise being pitched against further counter arguments. If it continues to survive, then it would be progressively strengthened with each attempt, based on the principle of the weight of accumulated evidence. It would always be susceptible to some new theory or discovery, but at least the topic has been researched in a systematic way rather than being neglected.

A word of warning, though. It would be all too easy to set up 'straw man' alternative arguments, that would be relatively simple to discount. This would serve no purpose, and would undermine the ethical integrity of serious scientific investigations.

If we can conclude, albeit tentatively, that the ability to enjoy music is an innate gift, then where does this gift come from? The answer, if indeed one is possible, will depend on your beliefs in a higher power being at work in the world. Piecing together opinions from several eminent researchers creates the following statement:

In all known civilisations, it has been believed that music had a divine origin, perhaps the only particle of the divine that humankind has been able to capture.

Some take this further, and think that it is the language of higher entities; it aspires to the harmony of nature and man, and is considered to be the gift of the gods. What do *you* think?

Chapter 17

The three-wheeled van

A car made famous by the BBC television comedy sitcom 'Only fools and horses', which made its debut in nineteen eighty-one and ran for ten years, was a three-wheeled Reliant van. The programme featured Derek 'Del Boy' Trotter, played by David Jason, as the market trader who used this jalopy as the business vehicle for his company: 'Trotters Independent Trading Co.' This did not prove to be the most reliable means of transport, and it brought back memories of a similar conveyance that I owned many years previously.

As a young lad, I was mad keen on being involved with any sort of motorised vehicle – a passion no doubt shared by many other boys and girls. In those days, not long after World War Two, owning a motor car was the exception rather than the norm. My parents did not have one until my age reached double figures, so it was useful to keep on good terms with the privileged few friends and neighbours who were independently mobile. Even if you did own a vehicle, petrol rationing severely limited its use. A local insurance agent even went so far as to buy a motorised bicycle, and used his more generous car petrol coupons when he bought fuel for it. This enabled him to cover the distances required for him to do his job, albeit it in less comfort than he was accustomed to.

A very nice man, who lived just a few doors away from us, had an interesting little car. It was a two-seater convertible, and the boot opened outwards to reveal what he called a 'dickey seat'. Provided you were not too large, and did not mind being out in the open, you could enjoy a ride even when both the inside seats were occupied. Whilst I cannot be certain of the model, looking through the vintage car list now, it resembled a pre-war Austin Seven Opal.

Whenever the owner was cleaning or tinkering with it, I was out there in a flash, just wanting to be involved with it in any way that I could. My presence was tolerated even if it was more of a hindrance than a help, and it was a joy upon joys when he took me on a little run to check that the car was working satisfactorily. Even the faint smell of petrol was, to me, like the fragrant perfume rising from the flowers in a meadow is to a bee.

In the earlier article: 'Do you remember the war?' it was mentioned that, when he retired, my grandfather Herbert bought The Manor House in Welton, near Lincoln. The property was set within a few acres of land that the family farmed. After the old man died, the estate was managed by one of my uncles. My own family used to visit him from time to time. On one of these little holidays I discovered that they had acquired a motorised plough. This was a strange contraption, with a pair of big metal wheels powered by a large engine that had to hand cranked into action using a starting handle. Two long handlebars stretched out behind, which the operator held onto as he walked, just like with a horse-drawn version

It was a versatile machine, as not only could it be used as a plough, but the cutting blade could be removed and the body then connected to a trailer. You could then sit on the edge of the cart and drive around the smallholding. Now and again I was allowed to steer this unwieldy transport for short distances across the field. Such bliss, to be actually driving a motor vehicle – it could not have been more enjoyable to a youngster like me even if it had been a Rolls Royce!

When I was aged about ten, my father bought a second-hand Ford 10 car; its registration number is still lodged in my memory: VH 9226. Each morning I was permitted to perform a ritual, which involved pushing it backwards out of the garage, filling up the radiator with water, and cranking the engine with the staring handle a few times. My father would then come out and start up the engine, if it in fact did start, which was not always the case. All being well, I was then dropped off at school.

Although it was enjoyable to have this involvement with the car, I did not of course have the opportunity to drive it. If my memory serves me correctly, my first encounter with a mechanical vehicle that I *could* operate myself was with a lawn mower. My father knew somebody who lived next to the Thames in London, and our family once spent a short summer holiday with them. They had a large lawn that stretched nearly down to the river. One day I heard the sound of a petrol engine starting up. Rushing out into the garden to see what was responsible for this exciting noise, I saw the host just starting to cut the grass with a motorised lawn mower. "Please, please may I have a go?" I said eagerly.

This was not something on which you could ride, but it was self-propelled and, to me who must have been aged twelve, a proper, grown-up mechanical device. The tolerant owner agreed that I could operate it, and he showed me what to do. Whilst it took literally several more years before understanding that clutches had to be let in slowly, I spent many a happy hour during this holiday jerking the clattering machine into motion and trotting along behind it. There is no doubt that the mower had to undergo some major repairs, once our family had departed and left the residents in peace.

Another five years passed before the opportunity came along to own a powered vehicle, and it was a case of starting on the bottom rung of the transport ladder. My father bought a very old moped for me from a neighbour. It was much like a pedal bicycle but with the addition of a small two-stroke engine, mounted low down in the centre, and which had a chain drive to the back wheel. A triangular tank for the fuel was bolted on to the frame above the motor. There were no gears, and it was started by peddling as fast as possible and then letting in the clutch via a lever on the handlebars.

If one managed to get it going, it chugged along at the stately pace of about fifteen miles per hour.

Although it was a thrilling experience to be conveying myself by mechanical means, the machine was in poor condition, probably made even worse by my attempts to tinker with it. After only a matter of days, the previous owner agreed to take it back. However, my return to pedal cycling did not last very long. My parents were still keen for me to have my own motor transport, especially as I had recently started work in a medical laboratory that was situated out of town. They bought me a small, single seat motorcycle.

Although not now remembering the make and model, a trawl through the Internet pages revealed that it was a black Excelsior 98 cc, hand-change, two-speed bike, made in the early nineteen-fifties. The Villiers engine was two-stroke, which means that oil and petrol were put into the same tank, and the two gears were changed using a small lever on the handlebar. The fact that it was not intended to go very fast was evident from the lack of a maker's speedometer, although a previous owner had fitted a basic gauge that was probably intended for a bicycle.

It was not trouble free. A problem with the spark plug oiling up and failing to fire was eventually resolved by slightly reducing the oil-petrol ratio to below the manufacturer's recommendation. Nevertheless, it provided much needed transport, and I even successfully took my driving test on this little motorbike. This meant that I was then able to drive anything with two or three wheels, provided it did not have a reverse gear, an engine above one litre, and an unladen weight exceeding five hundred and fifty kilograms. There was, therefore, an opportunity to move up in the transport world.

A three-wheeled car was an obvious choice, so my dad took me along to a dealer who sold Bond Minicars. For those not familiar with these vehicles, they have one wheel at the front powered by a 197 cc Villiers two-stroke engine, and two trailing wheels at the back. It was a convertible, with a bench seat for two people, and a tiny space behind for an extra passenger. These cars were very squat, being only about four feet high.

Although some of the later models had electric starters, for most of them the engine was started by pulling a long lever inside the cab as hard as you could. This was attached by a cable to what was probably a kick-start pedal by the engine. After several attempts, if you were lucky it burst into action. There were three forward gears, selected by using a control arm below the steering wheel.

We traded in the motor cycle for a second-hand model and, once the formalities had been completed, collected the Bond, giving me the opportunity to drive it home. This was the first of several three-wheeled vehicles I would have, and it felt good to be sitting behind the wheel playing chauffeur to my long-suffering father. But the joy was short-lasting. We did not have it for long, perhaps two or three weeks, as just about everything that could go wrong did so. My hands were blistered pulling the starting lever without success, having then to rely on a push start to get going – if indeed it ever did. Journeys where it broke down exceeded those where it did not. Oh dear, we had to take it back to the dealer.

For some reason my dad did not demand his money back but, instead, asked the manager what he had that we could take in its place. There was a motorbike and sidecar on the shop floor that had been taken in as part exchange, and we eventually agreed to have this. Although we were glad to have rid ourselves of the decrepit Bond Minicar, this meant that I would return to driving whilst being exposed to the elements, rather than being snug inside a little cabin.

This motorcycle combination must have kept me mobile for about two years and, compared with the previous vehicles, it was relatively trouble free. The machine was a very powerful Triumph Thunderbird 650 cc twin-cylinder four-stroke, which was quite a step up from the previous 98 cc bike, and even the 197 cc Bond. No one warned me about the need to lean sideways when making a turn, and there were a few hazardous moments when the sidecar wheel lifted alarmingly off the ground when trying to turn left!

As would be expected, the presence of the sidecar restricted the top speed to about 80 miles per hour, instead of the 100-plus the machine would have done solo. This extra weight also led to another problem. If the clutch had to be used continuously with this heavier load when crawling in heavy traffic, it quickly started to wear down. More than once I had to dismount and tighten the cable in order to keep going. Eventually, the vehicle started to show the effects of old age, and it was sold to a private buyer.

The proceeds were used to buy my first brand new means of transport, although it was a return to a solo motorcycle. Birmingham Small Arms Company (BSA) was famous for supplying 125 cc bikes to the Royal Mail for telegram delivery boys. These machines were in the characteristic Post Office red colour, and were produced in their thousands for over twenty years. The company then brought out a 'super' 175 cc model, and I took delivery of a shiny new blue one sometime around the year nineteen-sixty.

Driving off carefully on my first run, the engine seized up, bringing me to a sudden halt. Believing this to be my own fault for perhaps straying over the running-in speed, once it managed to re-start I made sure that the thirty mile per hour limit was not exceeded. However, the machine remained prone to seizing up like this for the whole of its time with me, which was very annoying. The only remedy was to leave it for a few minutes and then try to push-start it again. It was only when it was disposed of later that another dealer told me that he always skimmed a small layer of metal from the cylinder bore before selling these models, as he knew they had this problem. So much for British post-war workmanship!

The urge to have another attempt to find a three-wheeled car returned, especially as I played in a small band, and some form of conveyance was needed to transport the instruments. So, long before Trotter's Independent Trading came into being, I went in search of a Reliant Robin van. It took quite some time to find a second-hand model that was affordable on my limited budget but, eventually, one was located. After some haggling about the price, the BSA Bantam was part-exchanged for it, and I was told that it could be collected the next day once it had been checked over. When they saw it, my parents were less than happy that I had exchanged a newish motorcycle for this decrepit old banger!

On the 'plus' side, this particular example had had windows fitted to the side walls of the van. Under the regulations pertaining at that time, this meant that it was not restricted to the same slow speed limit as were those with solid sides. These vehicles had a conventional four-cylinder 750 cc engine, and four forward gears. What could be better than this – an ideal bandwagon that would take the lads anywhere! The old adage 'don't speak too soon' is an appropriate response. Add together all the problems experienced with my previous vehicles, double it, and you will have an inkling of what was in store for me.

It was not in my possession for more than a day before it became almost impossible to start. Before telephoning the dealer, I contacted the bank and asked them to stop the cheque that was used to pay the balance. This must have reflected badly on the dealer, because he immediately agreed to take the vehicle into the workshop and give it a thorough service. After this there was some improvement – but not for long. A fellow band member and I spent some time making it a bit more comfortable, including reinforcing the van floor and fitting some carpets at the front. It looked like we might at last have a serviceable vehicle.

There were just two things to remember. Firstly, it needed a pint of oil every time the petrol tank was filled. Secondly, the radiator kept boiling dry. The water was circulated not by a pump, but by a siphon system that worked on the principle that cold liquids sink and hot liquids rise. It was therefore assumed that the water would merrily find its way around the cooling pathways and keep the engine running at an optimum temperature. Whilst this idea is based on the laws of physics, the sudden overheating and seizing up of the engine was quite disconcerting when driving along a public highway.

One just had to remember to top up the radiator before a journey, and take a large bottle of water along in case of an emergency along the way. One evening, two band friends and I went to a concert in a town situated over thirty miles away. It was winter, and snow was on the ground. The journey was mostly along country roads without street lamps. Despite the very weak headlights (another challenge to be met with this vehicle) we made it to the venue, and enjoyed the entertainment. It was quite late at night when we set off on our return journey, and very few other cars were on the road.

About halfway home, the engine seized up and we skidded to a stop. Sure enough, the radiator was dry, but I had forgotten to bring the water bottle. There were no houses in sight, so we could not go and beg some water. All we could think of was to pick up snow from the roadside and push it into the radiator. Knowing that this material is only ten per cent water meant that we would need an awful lot of it to satisfy the thirst of this velocipede. Then one of the lads found an empty bottle. He decided to answer the call of nature in it, and add the contents to the radiator. Whilst not an ideal remedy, during an emergency one needs to think creatively.

When our hands were so numb that we just could not grab any more snow, I decided to risk driving off, hoping the engine would keep gong until we could find a house, preferably one with a light on. Luckily we did, and a very nice man let me have a can of warm water for the radiator. We then managed to get home without further incident, albeit very late at night.

A friend who was knowledgeable in things mechanical suggested that the engine would benefit from a major strip down, to see if its shortcomings could be remedied. Between us, we managed to do this but all we could find wrong was that one of the cylinders had a deep score mark. It was beyond our capabilities to do anything about it, so we just fitted new piston rings and re-assembled the engine. It did not perform much better, but my future wife and I made at least one trip to the coast in it. The only thing that went wrong then was that the fuel gauge stopped working. I managed to replace this, and it was then the most satisfactory part of the whole vehicle!

Eventually the van just had to find a new owner. A succession of cars followed, including an Isetta bubble car, and another Reliant three-wheeler – a more reliable one this time – before I obtained a full driving licence.

Then I could move up the scale and have my first four-wheeled vehicle. It was an old Ford 10, almost the same model as my father had owned many years previously. The fact that it jumped out of second gear unless you firmly held the lever in, was only a minor irritation. I have lost count of how many vehicles have been through my hands to date, but the one that will always stand out as being special – but not necessarily in a desirable way – is the Reliant three-wheeled van.

Chapter 18

Who was Melchizedek?

Melchizedek is a very shadowy figure who is briefly mentioned in the Hebrew Scriptures and the New Testament. Although the details there are minimal, to say the least, he also features in a number of ancient documents, including the Dead Sea Scrolls. If we are to believe the totality of what is written, our protagonist emerges as a very remarkable person indeed.

The first biblical reference to this individual is found in Genesis, chapter 14, verses 18 to 20. The wording in the New International Version (2011) reads as follows: "Then Melchizedek king of Salem brought out bread and wine [to Abraham]. He was priest of God Most High, and he blessed Abraham, saying, 'Blessed be Abram by God Most High, Creator of heaven and earth. And praise be to God Most High, who delivered your enemies into your hand.' Then Abram gave him a tenth of everything."

Abraham, or Abram as he was still known at that time, was returning home after defeating various kings in battle, and was camped just outside Jerusalem (previously called Salem). The king went out to meet him with the refreshments, and administered the blessing. This implies that Melchizedek was of superior status to that of the visitor, and this is supported by the fact that it was Abraham who paid tithes to him. Apart from adding that the king was a priest, it is surprising that we are given no other information about this obviously important person.

There is a brief reference in Psalm 110, listed as being written by King David. Verse 4 states, "The Lord has sworn and will not change his mind: You are a priest for ever, in the order of Melchizedek." Thus, great things were expected of David if he were expected to be an intermediary between God and the people, as was his role model. The psalmist obviously did not consider it necessary to clarify why this man should be regarded as worthy of such adulation, so his reputation must have already been well established and acknowledged. This just adds to the frustration of modern readers in their thirst for more information about him.

There is just one further mention of this enigmatic figure in the scriptures, and it appears in the New Testament over several verses of the book of Hebrews. Referring now to Jesus, the writer states that he: "Was designated by God to be a high priest in the order of Melchizedek" (chapter 5, verse 10). This same appellation is repeated several times in the verses that follow. Up until then, priests had to be descendents of Levi, and therefore from Abraham. It was expected that the promised Messiah would be a Levite, but Jesus was not; his earthly father could trace his ancestry back to David, and he was therefore a Judean. As a consequence, in order to justify his status, he was held as being 'in the order of Melchizedek' who, as we saw earlier, was superior to Abraham.

Chapter 7 mentions Salem and the meeting with Abraham, before it explains that the name Melchizedek means "king of righteousness" (verses 1-3). It then intriguingly states that he was "without father or mother, without genealogy, without beginning of days or end of life, resembling the Son of God." This statement is puzzling, and again it is not explained. Perhaps it is unsurprising that some regard Melchizedek as the Jesus of the Hebrew Scriptures (Old Testament), an immortal figure who came from God the Father and who will return there.

As the Bible does not give any further details about the life of this impressive man, perhaps assuming that everyone around at the time the scriptures were written would already be familiar with him, it is to other ancient sources that we must now turn. Firstly, what do we know about the dates of these events? Although scholars vary in their estimates, Abraham is believed to have been born in two thousand and sixty-six BCE, so Melchizedek's birth must have been at a similar time.

However, this would not be in keeping with the date of Noah and the great flood, which some say occurred nearly two hundred years earlier, in two thousand, three hundred and forty-eight BCE. As will be mentioned shortly, some sources state that our protagonist was involved in this natural disaster. Perhaps we should not worry too much about chronological accuracy, especially as Noah is reported to have lived for nine-hundred and fifty years!

The Old Testament Apocryphal text, *The Book of the Secrets of Enoch*, was written or edited in Egypt by an Hellenistic Jew some time around the beginning of the Christian Era. It tells of Melchizedek's birth. Due to the incredulity of the story, it is best that it is reproduced verbatim, as follows:

"And the wife of Nir, named Sopanima, being barren, brought forth no child to Nir. And Sopanima was in the time of her old age, and on the day of her death she conceived in her womb, and Nir the priest did not sleep with her, nor knew her from the day that the Lord appointed him to serve before the face of the people."

Nir thought his wife had been unfaithful, and banished her but, when the time came for the birth, he sent for her again. Sadly, Sopanima fell dead at her husband's feet. Nir, along with his brother Noe (presumably Noah) placed her on a bed, and planned a secret burial for her to avoid any shame. The narrative then continues:

"And then came an infant from the dead Sopanima, and sat on the bed at her right hand . . . and wiping its clothes. And Noe, and Nir were tempted with great fear, for the child was complete in its body, like one of three years old; and spake with its lips . . . . and lo! The seal of the priesthood was on its breast."

Thus we have a description of a virgin birth, but with the child being born shortly after its mother had died. He was dressed, and could walk and talk like a three-year-old. On searching for the meaning of 'the seal of the priesthood', one source (T. A. L. LeVesque *The Ancient Ones*) indicates that it was a large patch of scaly skin. There could also be horns and a tail. At least this is a description of Melchizedek's entry into the world, which does rather go against the statement in Hebrews about him having no beginning, even though it was a virgin birth. Does this sound familiar?

Keep in mind that these words were not penned until more than two thousand years after the alleged event, so it is possible that an element of embroidery has crept in to the narrative. Even the Genesis account was only written down – by Moses many believe – after a gap of over five hundred years. Stories from ancient times were usually preserved through oral tradition. This does not mean they were necessarily corrupted as they were passed on, but there is no way now of checking their accuracy.

The Enoch text continues by relating an interesting and quite detailed episode in the earlier life of Melchizedek. It transpires that a great lawlessness developed on earth, which is not elaborated but probably includes turning away from God. Nir became anxious, especially about the child, and believed that destruction was coming. He prayed to the Lord, and he was answered in a vision. God said that he would send a great destruction upon the earth, and every earthly creature would perish. But there was no need to worry about the boy, because he would send the Archangel Michael to take him to the Garden of Eden, where he would be safe. He would be proclaimed a 'priest of priests for ever.'

Noah and his family will also be preserved from the catastrophe (the flood), and they will settle somewhere else. The narrative then states: "another Melchizedek shall be head of the priests among the people . . . and the first king in the town of Salem."

Enoch not only describes our protagonist's beginning, but he also refers to his end – at least on this earth. Melchizedek will be a priest in the 'middle of the earth' where Adam was created, and he shall also be buried there. This account, and the book of Hebrews, were both written about the same time, that being in the early years of the Christian Era. Why then is there so much difference in the amount of detail related? Which are we to believe?

As mentioned earlier, there are also other ancient texts that refer to this mysterious

individual, among then the Dead Sea Scrolls. One fragment, 11Q13 (11QMelch) was written about one hundred years before the Christian Era, and deals mainly with the proclamation of the 'Jubilee'. Interestingly, the narrative includes several sentences or phrases that also appear in other books of the scriptures, including Leviticus, Deuteronomy, and Isaiah but, unlike the Scrolls, these are not specifically attributed to Melchizedek.

The Leviticus description contains the most detail. It states that a 'Jubilee Year' will take place each fifty years, and will be a time when all debts shall be cancelled, and all property returned to its rightful owners. In addition, those who are slaves, or are unfairly tied to contracts to serve their masters, shall be set free.

The Scroll version is incomplete, but includes the statement: "And from the inheritance of Melchizedek, who will return to them [the captives] what is rightfully theirs. He will proclaim to them the Jubilee, thereby releasing them from the debt of all their sins." Further on in the fragment are the words, "the Year of Melchizedek's favour, and by his might he will judge God's holy ones." It then adds, "He will deliver all the captives from the power of Belial."

In the year nineteen forty-five, some important documents known as the 'Gnostic Gospels' were discovered buried in the sand in Upper Egypt. They comprised thirteen leather-bound vellum bundles, dating from the second or third century of the Christian Era. Thus they are more recent than the other resources discussed so far in this essay, and they include references to Jesus Christ. They are collectively known as the *Nag Hammadi Library*, after the nearest town to where they were found. One of these has the title 'Melchizedek'. Unfortunately, the passage of time has led to deterioration of the writing, and there are many gaps in the text.

Near to the start, it states, "All the peoples will speak the truth who are receiving from you yourself, O Melchizedek, Holy One, High-Priest, the perfect hope and the gifts of life. Further on the man himself says, "I am Melchizedek, the Priest of God Most High; I know that it is I who am truly the image of the true High-Priest of God Most High." Clearly, he did not wish to leave his status in any doubt.

A little later he reveals yet another role, when he cites what somebody said to him:

"Be Strong, O Melchizedek, great High-priest of God Most High, for the archons [leaders] who are your enemies, made war; (but) you have prevailed over them . . . and you destroyed your enemies." We therefore now have a man who is not only a king and a priest, but also a successful warrior. It is apparent that, for hundreds of years, much was known about this remarkable individual, so all the more surprising that more details do not appear in the biblical writings themselves.

Yet there is still more to come. The Midrashim is the oral counterpart of the written Jewish Scriptures, and Professor Robert Hayward of the University of Durham discusses some traditions relating to our protagonist. He starts by confirming the status of both Abraham and Melchizedek as royal figures, and that they met at Salem (Jerusalem) where the latter was king, and was also regarded as being a Torah scholar.

The account then takes a different direction. The wine that was offered to Abraham was a bad omen. Israel's afflictions began when the two individuals met, and Melchizedek announced that the Jews would suffer and be enslaved by the Egyptian Pharaoh. Abraham was the one who emerged from this encounter as a hero. This is the only account seen so far that depicts our main character as a harbinger of doom.

The final document that was consulted, which is also the most recent, is *The Book of the Bee*. This is described as a Nestorian Christian sacred history, and was written around the year twelve hundred and twenty-two ACE by a Syrian bishop named Solomon. This sect originated about eight hundred years earlier, and it emphasises a distinction between the human and divine nature of Jesus. Section XX1 the bishop's book is entitled 'Of Melchizedek', and it tells a story somewhat different to those from the other sources.

Here, our subject is said to be the son of Mâlâh, who was a fourth generation descendent of Noah, and a mother named Yôzâdâk. Shem, Noah's son, took the boy "to the spot where the Lord was crucified, blessed him, and delivered him to the priesthood." He then said to him: "Thou shalt not drink wine nor any intoxicating liquor, neither shall a razor pass over thy head; thou shalt not offer to God an offering of beasts . . ." Shem then went back to his family, and wrongly reported that Melchizedek had died, and had been buried. The narrative later relates the story of the meeting with Abraham, and includes the statement: "And Melchizedek was honoured by them all, and was called 'Father of Kings.'"

There is something strange about the chronology of the Bee account. Firstly, there were apparently multi generations of Noah's family all active at the same time. However, there was a large degree of poetic licence about ages in those days. As was mentioned earlier, Noah was said to have lived for over nine-hundred years; his son Shem survived for six hundred years. Secondly, there is the mention of the place where 'the Lord was crucified'. Jesus only met his death more then two thousand years later, which is beyond the life-span even of the allegedly long-lived Noah himself.

It is time now to bring together what we know about the person who must have needed no introduction to the readers of either the Hebrew Scriptures or Christian New Testament. At the time these texts were written, Melchizedek could have been regarded as perhaps the highest spiritual being next to God, maybe even the 'Jesus' of the Old Testament' who was then reincarnated as the promised Messiah himself, as suggested in the New Testament.

Despite this, those who compiled the Bible took great care to incorporate only the most reliable texts in the final canon, but they must have found precious little to include about this revered individual. The sources that have been drawn upon for this essay may not have had the same level of authenticity as those in the Bible, but the fact that there are so many of them must indicate that he remained a person of significance.

To recap what the various sources have revealed, it is stated in the book of Hebrews (7:6) that Melchizedek was not descended from Levi (that being, the established priestly cast), but the implication is that he could nevertheless still trace his ancestry. Most of the apocryphal sources state that he came from Noah's family, either from his brother Nir, or a later relative. Hebrews also mentions that there is no record of his parents or ancestors, nor of his birth or death. However, the book of Enoch does describe his birth to a named earthly mother, although it was stated as being an immaculate conception. But we can be forgiven for regarding the description of him being born as a three-year-old boy, clothed, and able to walk and talk, as being over fanciful.

The Enoch text then states that Melchizedek was taken to the Garden of Eden to escape the flood, and several sources, including Hebrews, attest to him becoming King and High priest of Salem, and of his meeting with Abraham. One of his achievements was to proclaim a 'Jubilee Year' when debts would be cancelled and slaves freed. One source adds that he was also a successful warrior who defeated his enemies in battle. Although Hebrews states that nothing is known about his death, Enoch's account does mention that he will be buried in the middle of the earth.

There thus appears to be sufficient information to indicate that Melchizedek was a real person, and one who was highly regarded at time the various texts were written. Despite this, there are many gaps in the accounts of his life. He remains a mysterious figure around whom many myths and legends have arisen. This leaves ample opportunity for a writer to fill in the gaps and create an historical novel about him. This is just what led me to do in my book *Reincarnation*. It makes for interesting reading.

Chapter 19

Is hairdressing good for you?

This may seem to be a silly question to ask, but it was nevertheless the topic of a research project with which I was involved some time ago. As a part of their degree course, all third-year students are required to write a dissertation on a practical study they have carried out. In my capacity as a university lecturer in the department of psychology, each year I had several students to advise and supervise whilst they worked on their project. The first step is to discuss what topic the person wishes to investigate. Some already have a good idea what they want to do, whilst others need help. Ideally, it should be something that not only interests the individual, but is feasible – including having access to participants who will provide the data.

One of my male students had a girl friend who worked in a unisex hairdressing salon. He thought that this may provide an opportunity to conduct a survey among the men and women who visited the premises, on some aspect of having their hair cut or styled. We discussed various options relating to customer satisfaction, and the feelings associated with visiting the hairdressers. It was then necessary to consult reports of research carried out by others, to see what had already been investigated that had a bearing on this topic, and what options remained for a new study. It would serve little purpose to just duplicate something that had already been done.

There is much evidence available to show that we tend to favour other people whom we perceive as being physically attractive, because of the assumption that what is beautiful is also good. But does this also apply to our own self-image? Whilst this is not the only criterion we use to judge ourselves, it is indeed likely that both our physical abilities and physical appearance can have a marked effect on our feeling of well-being.

This raises another question, namely: does concern about self-image apply equally to both men and women? Results of previous studies have produced conflicting outcomes. One piece of research found that satisfaction with one's own figure was more important for women than it was for men, but another concluded that physical appearance had the greatest influence on men's self-esteem.

It might be expected that the importance we attach to how we look will vary with age and, according to some previous reports, this indeed appears to be the case. A survey carried out on a sample of young adults revealed that both genders were influenced by how they felt about their own body. Interestingly, the men were especially dissatisfied if their weight was below what they considered to be ideal, although on the whole the women were more figure conscious. However, the value that women place on their appearance is reported to decline with age.

What have researchers discovered about the importance people attach to their hair – the main topic of this essay, and one that is variously seen as a symbol of strength (the biblical story of Samson), sexuality, and magic? A relevant study had been carried out using photographs of women's faces. In some pictures the hair was masked out, and in others it was left visible. Although it is not surprising that the individuals were rated by others as being more attractive when the hair could be seen, when the trial was repeated with photographs of men, the opposite was found. In other words, men were rated as being *less* attractive when their hair could be seen, compared with when it was masked.

Before discussing the new study that the student and I carried out, there is a very relevant observation to share with you. In nineteen eighty-four, Jonathan Rabinowitz published an article in the *Child and Adolescent Social Work Journal* entitled, 'The Haircut: Its meaning in Childhood' Delving into history, he reported that travellers in ancient Egypt did not cut their hair until they had returned from their journey; and they then presented their cut locks as a gift to their god. In Greece, meanwhile, youths sacrificed their hair to the river. Apparently, in all cultures such offerings were regarded as being a substitute for the whole person.

However, Rabinowitz then stated that it is common for children to react to haircuts as if they were losing something of great value. Despite reassurances, and the lack of any pain or threat, they may become overwhelmed with terror. Why should this be so? A suggested answer emerges from the work of the psychoanalyst Sigmund Freud, who believed that hair can be representative of the male sexual organ, and that haircutting is, for boys, a symbol of castration.

Of course all this is in the subconscious but, if it is a credible hypothesis, we wondered if it could be carried forward into adulthood. If so, would this result in a dampened enthusiasm, especially among men, for haircutting? Could this then, in turn, inhibit the expected enhancement of self-esteem once the hair removal had taken place? In order to explore this, we devised some questionnaires to administer to the customers who visited the unisex hair salon.

After first carrying out a pilot study to test the validity and reliability of a selection of possible survey questions, we created two schedules, each comprising twenty items. These were designed to measure aspects related to self-esteem, such as how lucky a person considered themself to be, how good they felt for their age, and what their feelings were about their past and the future. Based on the findings from the pilot study, great care was taken to ensure that the two versions were as parallel as possible, and would result in very similar scores if they were administered at the same time.

Over a period of several weeks, visitors to the salon were asked if they would take part in the study. This continued until we had received completed questionnaires from one hundred customers, with equal numbers of men and women. Their ages varied from teenagers to those in their sixties. Participants completed one version of the questionnaire before they had their hair cut or styled, and the other version immediately afterwards. The only personal details requested were gender and age, otherwise the responses were anonymous. The 'before' and 'after' versions were clipped together, and returned to the University for processing.

Once received, the first step was to convert the responses to numbers, enter them into a computer spread sheet, and then analyse them using a powerful statistical programme. The benefit in having access to computerised analysis is that it takes the guesswork out of trying to decide if any differences in scores that are obtained, are significant or not. Research in psychology rarely, if ever, produces a hundred percent 'yes' or 'no' result. People are not machines or chemicals that are guaranteed to always react in exactly the same way every time. As was stated in a previous chapter, in the human sciences a result has to have at least a ninety-five per cent probability of being true, if it is to be regarded as meaningful.

We looked first to see if there were any differences in levels of self-esteem between the different age ranges of the customers, when tested before any hair dressing had taken place. Although there was a very slight indication that this does increase with age for women, but not for men, the finding was below the accepted level of significance. What we did find that was significant, was that the initial level of self-esteem was higher for women than it was for men. What is more, it showed an increase when tested again after the hair treatment, whereas the scores for men remained unchanged.

This is quite interesting, and appears to confirm that women see the hairdressing as enhancing their physical appearance, whereas men just regard a haircut as something that needs to be done from time to time. But could our findings also confirm the notion that having one's hair cut creates anxiety in young boys, and that this is subconsciously carried through into adulthood? Is the act of losing hair symbolic for men of losing their virility through the 'unkindest cut of all' – castration? If this is the case, it could be that the effect is only temporary. If we could have located the male participants a few days later and tested them again, would their self-esteem scores have been higher?

There are many factors that could have influenced our results, and perhaps too much credence should not be afforded the outcome. It may simply be the case that men do not associate hair with physical attractiveness in the same way that women do. One aspect that was not considered in our study was the social ambiance of the hairdressing salon. Women usually spend more time in the hairdresser's chair per visit than do men, and having a good chat with a friendly stylist can be pleasurable in itself. It is therapeutic to talk, and some studies have been carried out that do indeed confirm the useful role of the hairdresser as a counsellor.

Our investigation was completed several years ago. Informal observation of men in the barber shops since then suggests that many are now much more particular about their hairstyle and resulting appearance than they used to be. Trends may be started by male film stars or performers on the stage or television, which are considered desirable to copy, especially by the younger males. If we had to do this study again, would we now find that men's self-esteem was enhanced by a trendy hair style? On the other hand, would losing their hair still be symbolic of emasculation?

Chapter 20

What is heaven like?

In an earlier article: 'The meaning of life', I stated that a discussion on what happens when we leave this earth would be left for a later paper. Well, here it is. Assuming that there *is* a life hereafter – and some will say this is a very important assumption – what can we expect?

From time to time reports appear in the press from people who claim to have had near death experiences, and believe that they have glimpsed what heaven is like. One of the most detailed accounts in recent years was given in a book written by Dr Eben Alexander entitled *Proof of Heaven: A Neurosurgeon's Journey into the Afterlife* (Simon & Schuster, 2012). Alexander became ill with bacterial meningitis, and claims that he was brain dead for seven days, his body only being kept alive by a respirator. Whilst in this condition, he believes that he went on a journey into heaven.

To ensure his descriptions are accurately conveyed to you, here are some of his verbatim quotes. He started his journey in a place of pink-white clouds, before rising above them and saw: "flocks of transparent, shimmering beings arced across the sky, leaving long, streamerlike lines behind them." And then: "A sound, huge and booming like a glorious chant, came down from above . . . Seeing and hearing were not separate in this place."

He then introduces an intriguing new element. "For most of my journey, someone else was with me. A woman." After describing her beauty, he continues: "When I first saw her, we were riding along together on an intricately patterned surface, which . . . I recognised as the wing of a butterfly. In fact, millions of butterflies were all around us – vast fluttering waves of them." Returning now to the woman, he writes: "Without using any words, she spoke to me. The message went through me like a wind, and I instantly understood that it was true."

The message the woman 'spoke' was one of reassurance: "You are loved and cherished, dearly, forever. You have nothing to fear. There is nothing you can do wrong." Whenever he silently asked a question, "The answer came instantly in an explosion of light, colour, love, and beauty that blew through me like a crashing wave." This is all very beautiful, colourful and comforting. But what are we to make of this picture of paradise in heaven?

Most, if not all of the near death experiences reported by people, use similar glowing terms to describe what they encountered. A brilliant light is usually involved. Often there is a tunnel through which the 'dying' person is travelling, before being – in some cases reluctantly – pulled back to earthly life before they have reached whatever there is on the other side. Floating above one's body and looking down at it is a common occurrence. The British comedy star Peter Sellers once reported in a televised interview that he had had a heart attack, and 'died' for one and a half minutes. He said that, during this time, he knew that if he held on to a hand that had been proffered, he would then be able to return to life.

It is interesting that, like the experience of Eben Alexander, nearly all the accounts are very positive, with strong feelings of peace and love. Many encounters are distinctly religious, with Christian imagery, or of well-known artistic representations of these. In the face of the sheer number of examples reported, should we now conclude that that we have convincing evidence that heaven exists, and even an idea of what it is like? Much as we may wish this to be the case, unfortunately most claims do not withstand independent scrutiny.

Alexander's account has been discredited by those who treated him in hospital. They say that he was deliberately placed in an induced coma, and his brain certainly was not dead. The images he saw were regarded as hallucinations, rather than the result of an out-of-body experience. Many conditions can produce such images, including religious fervour, migraines, and social isolation. Anaesthetics often have side effects, as do other chemicals; flashing lights, colours, and feelings of detachment are not uncommon.

The reason that the visions seem so real is that the same neural mechanisms are at work as is the case with actual perceptions. Perhaps those images that depict what it is like when we leave this earth are the workings of an innate defence mechanism in our brain that helps us to avoid unnecessary worry about our ultimate fate.

Parapsychologists have set up experiments in hospital emergency treatment rooms to investigate claims that the soul can float above the physical body, and look down on it. Objects are placed on top of cupboards and shelves, so that they cannot be seen from ground level. If a patient is convinced that they have had an out-of-body experience and risen to the ceiling, they are asked what they saw on top of the furniture or shelf. So far, nobody has succeeded in correctly identifying any such item.

Despite the lack of hard scientific confirmatory evidence, these glimpses of the 'other side' are mostly peaceful and comforting, usually eliminating all concerns about the death that will ultimately befall. It would, therefore, be inappropriate to completely debunk these reports, provided they are genuine beliefs and not just fabricated in order to sell books. If they are real for the beholders, then we must leave them to enjoy the privilege they have had of looking into heaven.

Those who do believe that there is a life beyond our earthly one often struggle with some of the practical concerns of a heavenly existence. For example: 'Do we remain at the age we are when we die?' 'As the majority of those who die are elderly, is heaven just like a retirement home full of old people?' 'Will it not become over-crowded as more and more folk arrive there?' Such questions are quite understandable – if, that is, we think that heaven operates on similar lines to those on earth, except that when we are there we live in some eternal bliss with our loved ones who had arrived before or after us.

Whilst there can be no doubt that it will be a nice place in which to spend our days, once we have shed our earthly body, perhaps we should use a different line of thought when we try to imagine what it will actually be like. I tried to do this in my historical novel, *Reincarnation*, and I share some of my ideas with you here.

Firstly, where is it? My response is that there are many parallel universes – a possibility acknowledged by today's scientists. Some of these domains may be inhabited but, so far, we have little idea of what they contain. Heaven could be one of them. It is not, therefore, literally 'up there', but it is in a place complementary to where we are now, maybe even very close to us. We enter it by crossing the boundary into another realm. The journey will likely be quick – even instant – because time and space as we know it only operate in our present universe.

The next question might be: is there an actual Godhead, a being of some sort, which controls this heavenly place? In an earlier article, 'The meaning of life', I suggested that a secular idea of what was there before the universe began was that it was a mass of primordial energy. Those people with religious beliefs might prefer to put a shape to this and regard it as the 'Supreme Being' who was responsible for all creation. Whichever way you may wish to picture this initial power, it would seem reasonable to assume that it is still at work in the organisation and management of the place we regard as heaven. Its workings would be just too complicated for it all to be due to random happenings

My own vision, as described in *Reincarnation*, is of the controlling nucleus being a shining blue orb that radiates coloured particles of energy that bring feelings of great joy peace to all those it touches. The power of this entity is such that no one can approach right up to it to see the Supreme Being within, and live. This central body speaks to us through a process akin to thought transference, and we each hear the words in our own language. Likewise, we can communicate with it using just our minds.

Further questions might include, what does heaven look like? Well, my view is that, apart from the actual Godhead, it can appear to each individual as a utopia that encompasses everything he or she is personally comfortable with, or desires it to be. This includes not just what we see and feel, but also the sounds we hear – so important for music lovers – and even what we smell and taste. In other words, there is no fixed appearance – it is tailored to suit every individual's wishes.

The terrain may seem to be real and solid, but this is a spirit world and the substance exists only in mind of the beholder. Similar reasoning can address the concern that some may have that it is a world consisting mostly of old people? I suggest that this is not the case, but that we can see others, and ourselves, as being of any age that we wish. The laws of nature that we are used to on earth just don't apply in heaven.

Keeping this in mind, my response to the concern that heaven will become increasingly crowded as successive numbers of people die, is easy to articulate. With this being a universe devoid of physical matter, we may appear to be solid and made of flesh and blood but, in reality, we are just formless souls that take up no space. Not only that, but we originate from the creator Godhead, and then return to being a part of it when our mission on an earth-like planet is done. Thus, the total mass that makes up the central orb of energy and the spirits that come and go, remains constant.

Shall we see loved ones who have either predeceased us, or have followed later? Yes, I believe we shall have the joy of being reunited with them. And now, perhaps the biggest question of all – shall we all remain in this place for ever? How we wish to respond to this will depend on our view of reincarnation. Hinduism is a religion that believes in the transmutation of the soul, and that we progress through several existences until we achieve the goal of freedom from 'kārma' (causal action) and become part of the Divine Being itself. This is poetically likened to a river entering the sea, thereby losing its individual identity and becoming part of the greater whole.

Thus, for the Hindus and those who share a similar view, there will not be just one visit to heaven, but many. It is indeed tempting to think that we shall all be recycled, being absorbed back into the Godhead and then regurgitated to live a new existence. If there is any factual basis to claims made by people who are sure they remember a previous life – and this is by no means certain, as they can usually be explained in more mundane ways – then reincarnation could provide an explanation for them.

The final big question that is often asked is: do only good people go to heaven, whilst the evil ones are condemned to the fires of hell for ever? If you wish to seek for an answer in the Hebrew Scriptures or Christian Bible, you will find texts that lend support to both these alternate points of view. It all depends on how much of a Universalist you are – believing that all will ultimately be saved, compared with being a Particularist – that only the good, or those predestined to do so, will be achieve this.

Biblical passages that support the former include: "The Lord Almighty will prepare a feast for all peoples" (Isaiah, 25:6-8) and, "God, who is the saviour of all people" (1 Tim, 4:10). Examples of texts that suggest Particularism are: "Surely the day is coming; it will burn like a furnace. All the arrogant and every evildoer will be stubble" (Malachi, 4:1) and, "Depart from me, you who are cursed, into the eternal fire prepared for the devil and his angels." (Matt, 25:41). These are just a few of the many verses that point us either in one direction, or the other.

So, which of these views do you wish to follow? Are we all destined for heaven, regardless of how we behave on earth? As there is no ultimate consensus in the Scriptures, we need to rely on our own powers of reasoning to try and find a satisfying answer. My own conclusion agrees with that of one of the founding fathers of the Christian church, Origin of Alexandria, who lived from about the year one hundred and eighty-four until two hundred and fifty-two of the Christian Era. He believed that the wicked would be only temporarily separated from God, and that ultimately all things will be restored.

Does it seem reasonable to accept that those who have committed the most heinous of crimes, including being responsible for the cruel deaths of countless others, should have access to heaven, assuming there is such a place? It is right that they be punished for their sins, and also given time – perhaps a very long time – to repent. Eventually, however, there should come a point where they can seek forgiveness and have an opportunity to enter the gates of heaven.

Those of us who are fathers or mothers know that our children can, despite our best intentions and teachings, do wicked things, and even turn against us.

Should we therefore condemn them to everlasting punishment? A loving parent will always be ready to forgive, and will not abandon their offspring. If there is a God who is our spiritual father, then surely we shall also be loved and forgiven, and given the chance to redeem ourselves.

Can we now draw some conclusions about what heaven is like, assuming there is an afterlife destination to which we can give this name? Western artists often depict it as a colourful and peaceful utopian landscape, or maybe as fluffy white clouds inhabited by winged angels playing harps. But would a similar image be painted by someone living north of the Arctic Circle, or in the South American rain forest? Did those living two thousand years ago see heaven in this way? Will people who inhabit our world thousand years from now have a different image?

If each artist has been depicting what they think this paradise would be like, then they are all correct. Because my own view is that we shall experience an environment that will be individually perfect for us. There can be no fixed landscape – it will be what we each want it to be. Otherwise it would not be heaven, would it?

96761518R00147